PORTO
THE CITY AT A GLANCE

Alfândega
Eduardo Souto de Moura transfo
customs house into a congress ce
Rua Nova da Alfândega, T 22 340

Palácio da Bolsa
Take a guided tour of Porto's ne
stock exchange, finished in 191
the Moorish decadence of the ?
Rua Ferreira Borges, www.palac

Clérigos
The tower of Nicolau Nasoni's masterful
1763 church combines baroque exuberance
with the grandeur of a Tuscan campanile.
Rua de São Filipe Nery, T 22 200 1729

Praça da Ribeira
This central square was once a harbourside
market. Now it's a popular meeting place.

Sé do Porto
Behind the cathedral's imposing facade is a
delightful Romanesque and Gothic interior.
See p009

Hotel Dom Henrique
In 1973, this hotel became the city's first
concrete high-rise. Its asymmetrical shape
recalls Frank Lloyd Wright's Price Tower.
Rua do Bolhão 223, T 22 340 1616

Ponte Luís I
Gustave Eiffel associate Théophile Seyrig's
1886 bridge seems to fly across the Douro.
See p013

Mosteiro Serra do Pilar
In summer, there are concerts on the terrace
of this 17th-century monastery. The circular
domed church is also worth a visit.
Largo de Avis-Santa Marinha

INTRODUCTION
THE CHANGING FACE OF THE URBAN SCENE

Portugal's second city is a straight-talking, hard-working town that has always been proud of its mercantile heritage. It is a place of traders and the bourgeoisie and, as a result, there is little by way of grandiose urban set pieces. Indeed, much of Porto's attraction (and its UNESCO World Heritage site status) derives simply from the manner in which its humble granite houses cluster together picturesquely on the steep terrain. Many of the best contemporary buildings are the signatures of the globally lauded local architect Álvaro Siza Vieira (see p072), whose poetic but deceptively complex modernism is clearly inspired by these dramatic streetscapes.

The city has always been defined by its international harbour, after which it is named. When the port moved out to neighbouring Matosinhos in the 1970s, the centre lost a great deal of its prosperity, which it has taken a long time to recover. Now, though, a wave of interest spearheaded by an active arts and student community has re-energised Downtown with a vibrant cultural life unimaginable only a decade ago. The danger is that the authorities, desperate to clean up the historic old town, will scrub out much of its character, destroying a unique environment along the way. For the moment, however, Porto has an old-world vitality and a community spirit that is increasingly hard to find in a major European destination, and a new generation of architects, designers, restaurateurs and artists determined to keep it in sync with the rest of the world.

ESSENTIAL INFO
FACTS, FIGURES AND USEFUL ADDRESSES

TOURIST OFFICE
Porto Turismo
Rua Clube dos Fenianos 25
T 22 332 6751
www.visitportoandnorth.travel

TRANSPORT
Airport transfer to city centre
Line E trains depart every 10 minutes. It's a half-hour journey to Campanhã station
Car hire
Avis
Rua Guedes de Azevedo 125
T 22 205 5947
Metro
T 808 205 060
www.metrodoporto.pt
Trains run from around 5am-1am; the Yellow and Blue lines run 24 hours on weekends
Taxis
Raditaxis do Porto
T 22 507 3900
Radio Taxis Os Unidos
T 22 502 9898
There are ranks on Rua dos Clérigos and outside São Bento station. It is safe and easy to hail cabs on the street

EMERGENCY SERVICES
Emergencies
T 112
Late-night pharmacy
www.farmaciasdeservico.net
Check the rota online

CONSULATE
British Consulate
Rua de São Bernardo 33
Lisbon
T 808 203 537
www.ukinportugal.fco.gov.uk

POSTAL SERVICES
Post office
CTT
Praça General Humberto Delgado 320
T 707 262 626
Shipping
FedEx
Rua do Barreiro 553
T 22 943 6034

BOOKS
Álvaro Siza: The Function of Beauty by Carlos Castanheira (Phaidon Press)
Hunting Midnight by Richard Zimler (Constable & Robinson)
Journey to Portugal by José Saramago (Vintage)

WEBSITES
Architecture
www.arquitecturanoporto.blogspot.com
Newspaper
www.theportugalnews.com

EVENTS
Fantasporto
www.fantasporto.com
Open House Porto
www.openhouseporto.com

COST OF LIVING
Taxi from Francisco Sá Carneiro Airport to city centre
€20
Cappuccino
€1.50
Packet of cigarettes
€4
Daily newspaper
€1
Bottle of champagne
€80

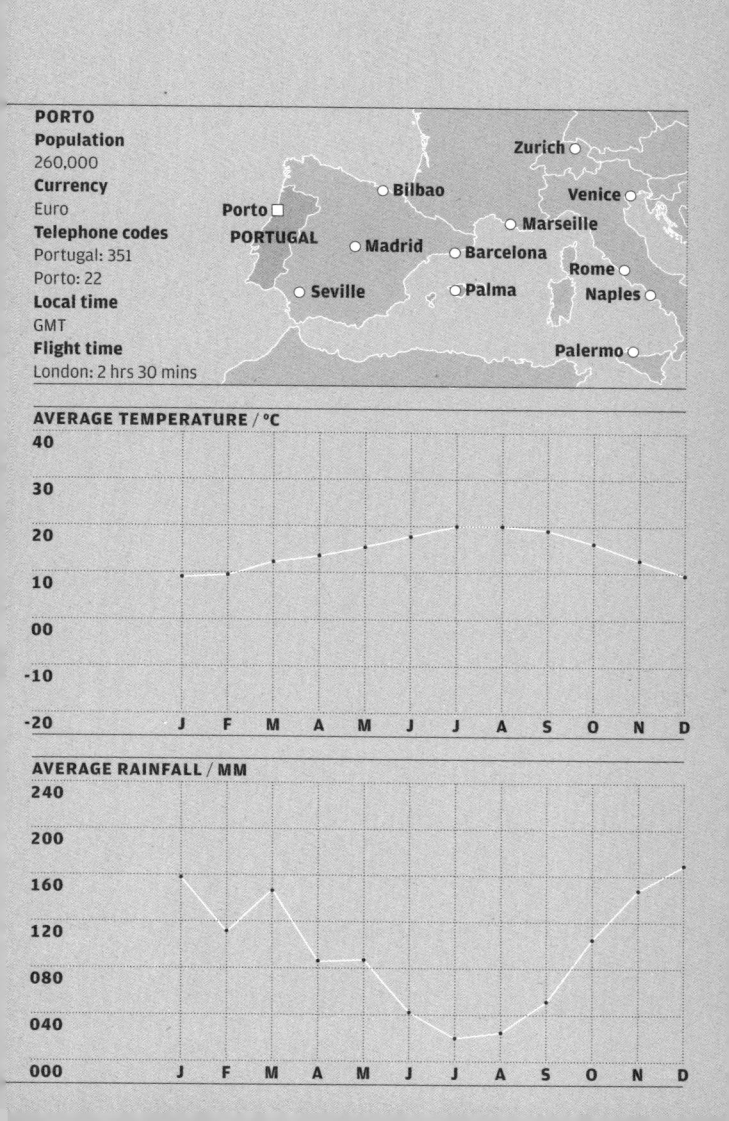

PORTO
Population
260,000
Currency
Euro
Telephone codes
Portugal: 351
Porto: 22
Local time
GMT
Flight time
London: 2 hrs 30 mins

AVERAGE TEMPERATURE / °C

AVERAGE RAINFALL / MM

NEIGHBOURHOODS
THE AREAS YOU NEED TO KNOW AND WHY

To help you navigate the city, we've chosen the most interesting districts (see below and the map inside the back cover) and colour-coded our featured venues, according to their location; those venues that are outside these areas are not coloured.

MATOSINHOS
The port relocated here to an enormous container facility in the 1970s, though the atmosphere remains sedate. Visit for the top seafood eateries, such as Salta o Muro (Rua Heróis França 386, T 22 938 0870), and to pay homage to architect Álvaro Siza Vieira – his Piscina das Marés (see p080) is a delight – in the place of his birth.

FOZ DO DOURO
Urbane and leisurely, Foz has long been Porto's sophisticated beach playground. The neighbourhood's wealth is visible in the mansions that line the coastal road and its heavyweight restaurants, such as Pedro Lemos (see p032). However, Foz has been overtaken by Baixa as the city's hippest nightlife and commercial zone.

BOAVISTA/CEDOFEITA
OMA's Casa da Música (see p010), built on the site of a tram depot, is prominently situated on Avenida da Boavista, a grand 19th-century boulevard that gives this part of town its name. Many of Porto's chicest shops are to be found here, including the menswear gem Wrong Weather (see p094).

SANTO ILDEFONSO
This residential 'hood rises from the retail hub of Rua de Santa Catarina, yet retains a villagey vibe. Santo Ildefonso is a fine baroque church, but it's the hulking great Silo-Auto (see p014) that dominates the area. Simple *tascas* (snack bars) abound.

LORDELO DO OURO/SERRALVES
The Serralves Foundation (see p068), with its gardens and contemporary art gallery, is the dominant attraction here, despite its setting amid swathes of monotonous 20th-century housing. Far more appealing is the riverfront, from where the Flor de Gas ferry carries passengers across the water to the pretty fishing hamlet of Afurada.

CLÉRIGOS/DOWNTOWN
Downtown was long considered obsolete in comparison with the affluent suburbs. But since the financial crisis, an effort has been made to reinstate Clérigos, with its steep streets and historic buildings, as the centre of the city's social life. Don't miss the museum-piece diner Confeitaria Cunha (Rua Sá da Bandeira 676, T 22 339 3070).

MASSARELOS
Once home to the bourgeoisie, Massarelos is still underpopulated and genteel, except for the riverside. Many of its estates were claimed by the state and are now home to university faculties (see p084) and the Jardins do Palácio de Cristal, where you'll find chef Vitor Matos' Antiqvvm (see p088).

GAIA
Facing Porto from across the Douro, Gaia is famous for its wine cellars, located here as the southern riverbank is less prone to extreme temperatures. East of Ponte Luís I, you'll discover semi-rural housing and the hilltop Mosteiro Serra do Pilar (see p009).

LANDMARKS
THE SHAPE OF THE CITY SKYLINE

Maps of Porto give little indication of its harsh topography and sheer cliffs. For the best overview of the city and to establish your bearings, head to the terrace at the Mosteiro Serra do Pilar (Vila Nova de Gaia) for its splendid sweeping vistas. What you will notice immediately are Porto's famous bridges – although the prettiest, Ponte Maria Pia (see p013), will be out of view – along with the central square, Praça da Ribeira, the wine cellars of Gaia south of the Douro and the charming Guindais and Fontainhas districts.

Look for the huge green dome of Pavilhão Rosa Mota (see p085) and follow the skyline east to the baroque tower of Clérigos (Rua de São Filipe Nery, T 22 014 5489), historically used by ships as a beacon, Sé cathedral (Terreiro da Sé, T 22 205 9028), austere from the outside, but with wonderful tiled cloisters, and the Coliseu (see p076), which is a feast of pink and neon at night. City Hall (Praça General Humberto Delgado, T 22 209 7135), a baroque pastiche, is at the top of Avenida dos Aliados, where Portuenses amass in times of both celebration and protest. This boulevard, near the beautiful São Bento station (see p072), forms the civic heart of the city.

Heading away from the centre, the wide Avenida da Boavista, flanked by Casa da Música (overleaf) and Torre Burgo (see p012), leads to the Atlantic suburbs of Foz and Nevogilde, and beyond to the port and seafront district of Matosinhos (see p073).
For full addresses, see Resources.

Casa da Música

OMA's asymmetrical performance hall is spatially rich and materially exuberant, and had a big impact on local architects, not to mention the city itself, when it was opened four years late in 2005. Up until then, Porto's design orthodoxy had been firmly in the Siza Vieira mould, but Rem Koolhaas and Ellen van Loon's complex forms and interior detailing – enormous scalloped glass curtains and gold leaf on wood – inspired a new expressiveness. The concrete hulk houses two concert halls, one at the scale of an orchestra and the other more intimate, wrapped in a winding series of circulation and social spaces. Visit the chequered roof terrace and the VIP room, which is a riff on traditional azulejo-tile interiors.
Avenida da Boavista, T 22 012 0200, www.casadamusica.com

011

LANDMARKS

Torre Burgo

Eduardo Souto de Moura, a protégé of the Porto School (see p072), has always had a soft spot for Mies van der Rohe, and this 2006 Burgo office complex is a fulsome tribute. Two buildings, one squat and the other soaring, sit on a podium together with a sculpture by the acclaimed late Porto artist Ângelo de Sousa, a typically abstract musing on form and colour. The ensemble is formally simple and internally unremarkable; all the interest lies in the facade, which is barely even disturbed by the entrance. Steel modules are stacked to create repetitive forms, with the glazing set deep. The 70m tower is a formidable presence in a part of the city where a clutch of new-builds evoke little inspiration, and is the first significant high-rise to have gone up near the centre since the 1970s.
Avenida da Boavista 1773

Ponte Maria Pia
Predating the more famous Ponte Luís I, which looms over Ribeira, Ponte Maria Pia is the unmistakable work of Gustave Eiffel, and was the first railway crossing over the Douro when it was finished in 1877. Luís I arrived a decade later, and was designed by Théophile Seyrig, who was an associate in Eiffel's firm. Maria Pia is the more graceful of the two. An elegantly arched wrought-iron structure, it was the longest bridge of its type in the world when it opened. It is only wide enough for a single track, yet it carried train traffic across the water until 1991. Since then, it has lain idle. After reports of metal rivets falling off into the river, the bridge was repaired in 2009, with a plan to open it as a pedestrian and cycle route – unfortunately the idea stalled.
Avenida de Gustavo Eiffel

014

Silo-Auto

Porto has never had any qualms about inserting huge car parks into its polite urban fabric; the art deco Maus Hábitos (see p047) dates from the 1930s. João Abel Bessa and Alberto José Pessoa's 1964 Silo-Auto building is a mammoth sculptural cylinder of bare concrete in the rectilinear city centre, a brutalist version of New York's Guggenheim.
Rua de Guedes Azevedo 148-180

HOTELS
WHERE TO STAY AND WHICH ROOMS TO BOOK

For decades, Porto's finest hotels were located in Boavista and Foz. The reawakening of Downtown has led to a proliferation of new and revitalised ventures, many of which more than compete with the established properties. Long-time favourites like the grandiose Infante Sagres (Praça Dona Filipa de Lencastre 62, T 22 339 8500) and Pestana Vintage (Praça da Ribeira 1, T 22 340 2300) have had lavish renovations. More significantly, entrepreneurs are radically transforming existing buildings to create design hotels, from the intimate Malmerendas (opposite) to Rosa et Al (see p018) – both without equal among Porto's small, central offerings. In Gaia, The Yeatman (Rua do Choupelo, T 22 013 3100) arrived in 2010 and has rooms overlooking the Douro, while the hulking Bolsa do Pescado has been imaginatively reused by the Vincci group (see p038).

If you're looking for more of a business-oriented option, some of the hotels in Boavista remain world-class, notably the Sheraton (Rua Tenente Valadim 146, T 22 040 4000) and plush Porto Palácio (Avenida da Boavista 1269, T 22 608 6600). The latter can boast the city's best Japanese restaurant, Góshò (Avenida da Boavista 1277, T 22 608 6708), in its basement food court, a stunning rooftop bar and a Pedro Cabrita Reis sculpture set in its courtyard. The Palácio do Freixo (see p023), a luxurious slice of history, is still extremely hard to beat if you are seeking to escape the urban milieu.

For full addresses and room rates, see Resources.

Malmerendas

This hotel exemplifies Porto's new breed of boutique accommodation – a classic 20th-century townhouse that still shows off its original features (large windows, wooden floors and decorative structural elements), updated with sleek, Scandi-influenced furnishings. The owners João Almeida and Joana Coelho partnered with architects Pedra Líquida on the five suites, offsetting the building's heritage with homey pieces that conjure up Arne Jacobsen and his ilk. The spacious rooms, each with its own kitchenette, mean that a night or two here feels more like staying in a friend's apartment than a hotel – it's a welcome respite from the city's chains. The Superior King Suite (above) is the pick of the bunch, with a dining area and balcony.
Rua Doutor Alves da Veiga, T 925 617 444, www.malmerendas.com

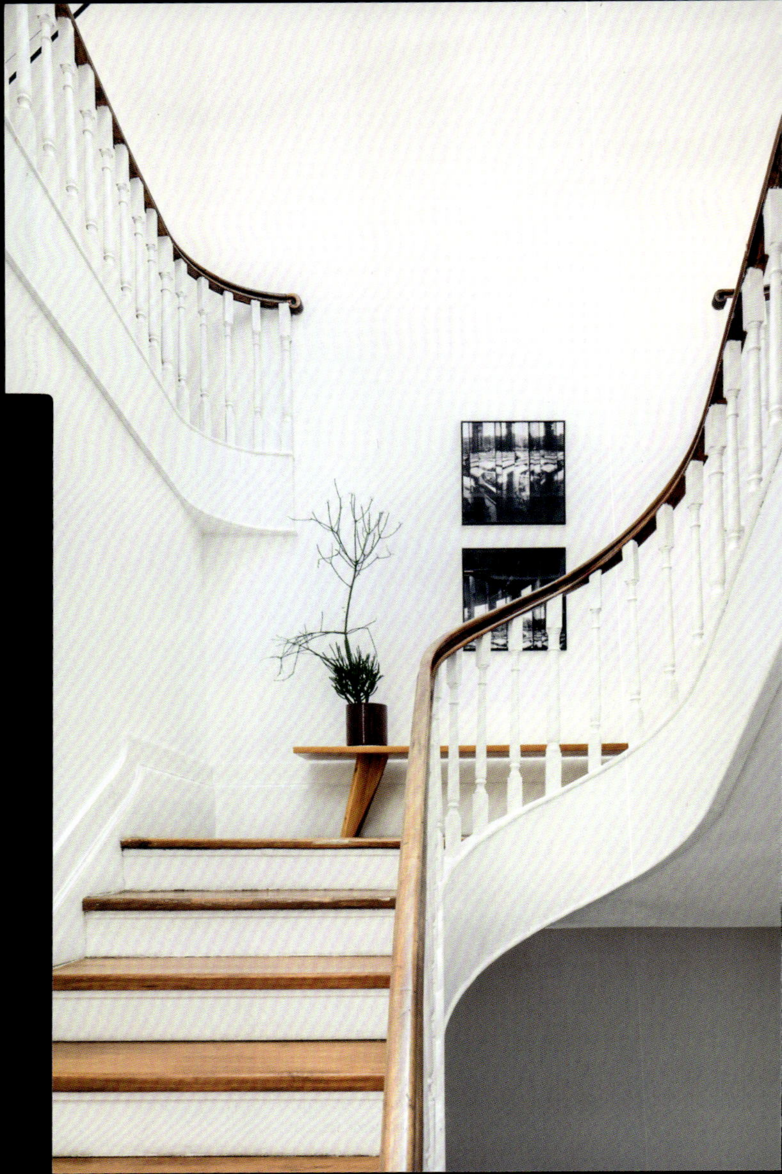

Rosa et Al

Since architect Emanuel de Sousa and his sister Patrícia rescued this three-storey townhouse in 2012, Rosa et Al has become a hotspot in the city centre, and a hit with Portuenses for its garden brunches and cooking classes. The property features an original domed skylight that crowns the staircase (opposite), and pieces from Jean Prouvé and Hans J Wegner help complete the difficult-to-obtain feel that the rooms here have hardly been designed at all. The Queen Deluxe City Heritage Suite (above) has a huge claw-foot tub and ornamental plasterwork ceilings. The Garden Pavilion, which has a pretty patio, arrived in 2016. Amenities have a local flavour – there are Castelbel products, and neighbourhood roasters Vernazza provide the coffee.
Rua do Rosário 233, T 916 000 081, www.rosaetal.pt

Pensão Favorita
A collaboration between the owners Ema Xavier and Filipe Maia, the architect Nuno Sottomayor and the designer Sam Baron, the Favorita opened in 2010 as a 12-room oasis in the Bombarda arts district (see p056). Within a beautifully restored 19th-century townhouse, it marries wooden floors with an unobtrusive colour scheme, impeccably selected Danish modernist furniture and an art collection curated by Júlio Dolbeth and Rui Santos of the Dama Aflita gallery (Rua de Picaria 84). Opt for either the spacious Room 5 (above) or one of the suites at the south-facing rear of the building, in particular Room 6, which has a terrace overlooking the garden. Nearby grocer/café Mercearia do Rosário (T 22 201 0504) is a fine option for a relaxed lunch.
Rua Miguel Bombarda 267, T 22 013 4157, www.pensaofavorita.pt

HOTELS

Casa 1015
This self-catering property was designed by none other than Pritzker prize-winner Eduardo Souto de Moura, and is a singular choice for architecture buffs. The house sleeps up to six people, and consists of two twin volumes that extend from a pair of intimate interior gardens. The building is set on a winding street in well-heeled Foz, and amalgamates a range of materials to strong effect – the original stone masonry of the exterior wall is a vivid contrast to the smooth concrete annexe, for example. Inside, the rooms are daubed in soft tones, although the choice of furnishings does feel a little aseptic. However, there's a slick melding of outdoor and indoor spaces, so we can forgive a little grey. The Mercearia do Miguel (see p035) is best for supplies.
Rua Padre Luis Cabral 1015, T 932 650 172, www.casa1015.pt

Palácio do Freixo

One of the reasons to visit the sprawling eastern suburbs, the Palácio do Freixo is an 18th-century baroque palace on the banks of the Douro, designed by Nicolau Nasoni, the Italian-born creator of many of Porto's civic and religious buildings. In 2000, Fernando Távora (see p072) treated the grand pile to a sympathetic restoration, to house the restaurant, bar and a gilded lounge, and also gutted the former flour factory next door in order to provide 87 elegant bedrooms (420, above). The two buildings are united by an outdoor pool and a series of terraces that leads down to a tented pier on the river. The aesthetic of the accommodation block has a somewhat corporate feel; the real stars here are the palace itself and the cascading gardens.
Estrada Nacional 108, T 22 531 1000, www.pestana.com

24 HOURS
SEE THE BEST OF THE CITY IN JUST ONE DAY

Start your day the traditional way with coffee and *pastéis de nata* in one of Porto's bustling cafés – try Bolhão (opposite), Confeitaria Império II (Rua de Fernandes Tomás 775, T 22 340 6187) or Mengos (Rua de Santa Catarina 161, T 22 200 3194). Then head to the upper level of Ponte Luís I (see p013) for the panorama before winding your way down to the river via the Barredo steps. Porto is not an easy city to walk around but it is an exciting one – the old town is a labyrinth of alleys, steep inclines and surprising vistas, the most beautiful examples of which are reachable only on foot.

The area around Miguel Bombarda is a shopper's delight – the Centro Comercial Bombarda (Rua Miguel Bombarda 285, T 934 337 703), for instance, is an ad-hoc assemblage of retail spaces in which you can find anything from vintage clothes to design objects. Now it's time to head to the coast. Catch a taxi to Matosinhos, and ask your driver to follow the river for the scenic drive. In summer, go for a dip in the Piscina das Marés (see p080) before a leisurely lunch in Casa de Chá (see p027). Afterwards, spend the afternoon amid contemporary art at Fundação de Serralves (see p068).

End the day in Downtown. Settle in at Miss'Opo (see p030) or try for a seat at Mondo Deli's communal table (see p033), ahead of bar-hopping between hip haunts such as Passos Manuel (see p047) and Galeria de Paris (Rua Galeria de Paris 56, T 22 201 6218). *For full addresses, see Resources.*

09.30 Confeitaria do Bolhão
This is the quintessential Porto breakfast spot, and it offers a spectacular selection of *fabrico próprio* (homemade) cakes and pastries. From the street, it looks like little more than a well-stocked bakery, but at the rear you'll find a spacious and handsome café, just one of many laidback eateries in the centre of town where locals meet up to gossip, and debate and dissect the events of the Brazilian soap operas that air on local TV. The Bolhão began life in 1896 as a favourite haunt of the bourgeoisie. But it has been cheerfully claimed by the people, particularly so since a major refurbishment in 1995, although we're still upset that the twinkling lights that were once set into the moulded ceiling were summarily replaced with a series of rather garish neon tubes.
Rua Formosa 339, T 22 339 5220,
www.confeitariadobolhao.com

11.00 A Vida Portuguesa

This nostalgic boutique sells traditional Portuguese products – including many that were previously discontinued – in packaging unchanged for decades. The brainchild of journalist Catarina Portas, the store is set within a former textile emporium that dates from the mid 19th century. The interior features bespoke cabinetry and a spectacular mahogany staircase (above). Older locals pick up fondly remembered childhood toys, well-designed cookware and food items, while younger customers are surprised to learn that something homegrown can be so cool. Some artefacts may lose their magic once out of the shop, though you can't go wrong with the Claus Porto toiletries and Lisbon-based stationer Emílio Braga's notebooks.
Rua Galeria de Paris 20, T 22 202 2105, www.avidaportuguesa.com

13.30 Casa de Chá da Boa Nova

Sublimely situated on the rocky coast of Matosinhos, this 1963 teahouse/restaurant was Siza Vieira's first major work, and it makes a fascinating comparison with the extension to Serralves (see p068), which was built 36 years later. Boa Nova melds vernacular details, such as immaculately crafted afzelia wood panelling, with a refined spatial quality that's reminiscent of Alvar Aalto or Frank Lloyd Wright. Have a glass of *vinho verde* (young white wine) in the intimate tea salon before sampling chef Rui Paula's cooking (see p096) in the restaurant (above), which is popular with Portugal's political elite. We'd order a bowl of *gambas* (prawns) and the house speciality *arroz de tamboril* (monkfish risotto). Or try the decadent eight-course tasting menu, which is an ode to shellfish. *Avenida da Liberdade, T 22 995 1785*

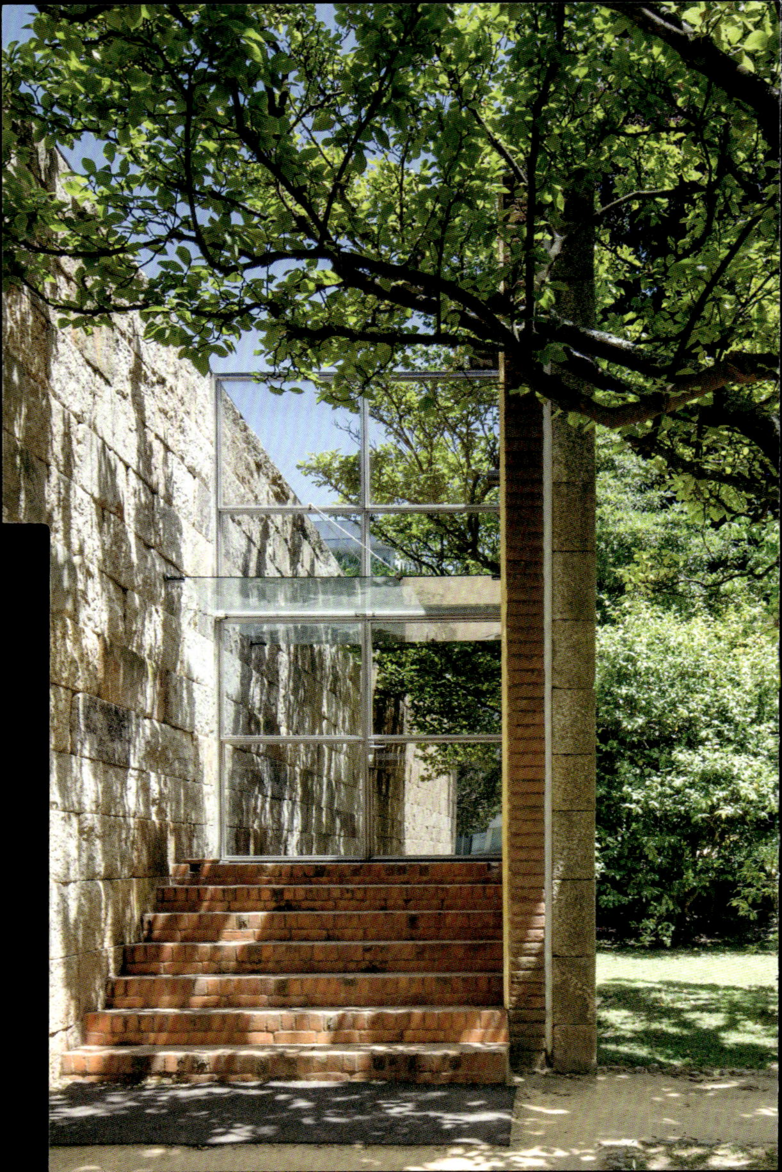

16.30 Casa das Artes

Located within the grounds of Casa Allen, a neoclassical 1920s pile that was originally built for the Belgian consul to Porto, Casa das Artes was the first large-scale project undertaken by now-starchitect Eduardo Souto de Moura (see p072), and finished in 1991. The cultural venue is understated almost to the point of anonymity from the exterior, its concrete, brick and glass fully integrated into an existing granite wall. The central hall (above) is used for exhibitions, and off it lead two rooms, one for cinema screenings (mainly cult and art house) and the other an auditorium for performances by young talent from the Iberian classical music scene. The best time to visit is during the summer season, for alfresco concerts hosted in the idyllic English-style gardens. *Rua Ruben Andresen 210, T 22 011 6350, www.casadasartes.pt*

21.00 Miss'Opo

Consisting of a café, bar and restaurant, Miss'Opo occupies the ground floor of a small, minimalist guesthouse (T 932 925 500), and has been drawing a happening crowd since 2012. The decor showcases local design talent: the delicate pendant lights were created by owner Paula Lopes in collaboration with architect Gustavo Guimarães; a Scandi-influenced cabinet is by Piurra (see p056); and tableware comes from Vista Alegre and Bordallo Pinheiro. Guimaraes' interiors retain a raw, industrial feel, warmed by vintage chairs and tables, and potted plants. The menu is nurturing and unfussy; there's often ceviche in the warmer months and *feijoada* (bean stew with smoked meat or seafood) in winter. On Thursdays, DJs spin in the main room.
Rua dos Caldeireiros 100, T 22 208 2179, www.missopo.com

031

24 HOURS

URBAN LIFE
CAFÉS, RESTAURANTS, BARS AND NIGHTCLUBS

It used to be that anyone in central Porto seeking a big night out would have had to take a taxi to one of the peripheral superclubs located somewhere on an industrial estate. Plenty of these places still exist, but they are no longer cutting-edge, as the Portuenses have rediscovered Downtown as the heart of the city's social life. The epicentre of this scene shifts with the breeze, from the early pioneers such as Passos Manuel (see p047), east of Avenida dos Aliados, to the newer venues west of it, like Miss'Opo (see p030) and hip music spot Café au Lait (Rua Galeria de Paris 46).

Porto has always specialised in beautiful cafés, from the belle époque Majestic (Rua de Santa Catarina 112, T 22 200 3887) to the 1950s Ceuta (see p052). The danger of the current flurry of regeneration in the centre is that it will sweep away these slices of history, so it's a blessing that sensitive renovations, in particular those at Café Vitória (see p042) and Café Candelabro (see p053), serve as examples of how to maintain architectural character.

Previously, all the best restaurants were located out near the ocean. It is still worth the trip to Pedro Lemos (Rua do Padre Luís Cabral 974, T 22 011 5986) and D'Oliva al Forno (Rua Brito e Cunha 354, T 22 935 1005) but upstarts Cantinho do Avillez (see p041) and Traça (see p045), among many others, are proving that inventive plates are not the sole preserve of affluent suburbanites. *For full addresses, see Resources.*

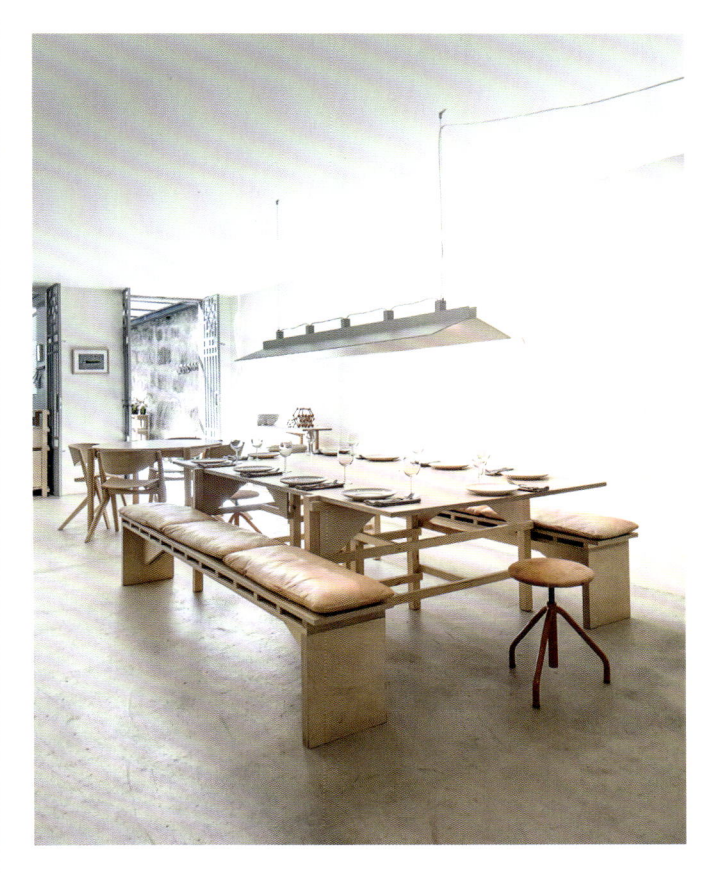

Mondo Deli

Established by Marcus Zietz and designer Christian Haas in 2016, this fashionable restaurant also doubles as a shop selling stylish products ranging from Japanese kitchen tools to jewellery by Saskia Diez. In a polished, convivial space, the kitchen serves up fusion-led tapas melding local flavours with those of Asia, the Med and Middle East. Inventive vegetarian plates, which might include charred aubergine with buttermilk, thyme and pomegranate dressing, are flush with spice and freshness. The wine list champions small production runs – perhaps try a drop from Quinta de Tourais in the Douro. Interiors, featuring custom-made furniture by Haas, are a sleek harmony of concrete, blondewood, leather, powder-coated steel and exotic plants.
Rua do Almada 501, T 22 203 3084, www.mondo-deli.com

Avenida 830

Isabel Neves opened Avenida 830 in 2016. The slender restaurant exudes a casual-chic ambience through neutral tones and minimalist furniture. A lovely rear patio is similarly uniform, anchored by an abstract colour-block wall and concrete fountain. Although Neves has no formal training in a commercial kitchen, she consistently sends out dishes whose good value belie the experimental flavours at play – the swordfish with sweet potato puree and passion fruit dressing is a true revelation. There are the classics too, such as *polvo à lagareiro* (octopus cooked with potatoes and drizzled with plenty of good olive oil). Pit stop here after visiting nearby Casa da Música (see p010); or it is a short walk to Siza Vieira's Bairro da Bouça (see p074). *Avenida da Boavista 830, T 962 374 478, www.avenida830.pt*

Mercearia do Miguel

This café/delicatessen, housed in a small building clad in aquamarine tiles that calls to mind a seaside bungalow, has operated as a grocer since 1958. On the walls, old photographs pay homage to the former proprietor, Sr Miguel, who collaborated with architect Nuno Felgar and designer Teresa Valle – the new owners – on this latest incarnation, which opened in 2013. Situated in Foz, it's an unbeatable spot for breakfast. Order an espresso and thick-cut toast with homemade jam, or granola served with açaí and seasonal fruits, and drink in the Atlantic views. Lunch is equally simple and tasty – tuck into a sandwich of *presunto* (dry-cured ham), artisan cheese, pesto and rocket – or swing past later on for a late-afternoon Sovina craft beer.
Rua do Passeio Alegre 130, T 22 011 6889, www.merceariadomiguel.com

Rádio

Promoter Pedro Salazar's bar occupies a spacious two-storey townhouse that was previously a car mechanic's garage, and the interiors are stripped back, simple and clean. A polished concrete floor runs throughout and corrugated cement panels line the walls. At the back is a large dance area that is clad in multicoloured timber, as well as Rádio's best feature – the leafy courtyard. Great attention has been paid to the toilet blocks: primary-hued 'pods' pitched somewhere between Archigram and Joe Colombo. Upstairs (right), the vibe is much more intimate. The custom-made furnishings are minimal and modern amid original decor details, like wooden flooring and soaring windows. Before you hit the tiles, the top-notch steak tartare with frites at nearby Brasão Cervejaria (T 934 158 672) will keep you going into the small hours.
*Praça Dona Filipa de Lencastre 178,
T 936 320 033*

URBAN LIFE

Vincci bar

Architect Januário Godinho's 1934 ocean liner of a building, with its cubist take on art deco, had been left to crumble until the Spanish hotel group Vincci acquired it, entirely overhauling the pile in 2015. Formerly a fish market, a fridge factory, a social centre and a nursery school, it now houses 95 guest rooms, a gym and a roof terrace with views of the Atlantic. But it is the mezzanine lobby bar (above) and ground-floor restaurant, 33 Alameda, serving refined native cuisine, which are the real highlights here. Local firm José Carlos Cruz has brought back the grandeur and exuberance, and the soaring arched ceilings are offset by sensuous 1940s-style interiors. Order the house cocktail, which is a mix of port, white rum and cinnamon.
Alameda Basílio Teles 29, T 22 043 9620, www.vincciporto.com

Cafeína

Located just a block away from the beach, Cafeína has been *the* neighbourhood spot for Porto's who's who crowd for a couple of decades. The turn-of-the-century edifice is clad in bold yellow-and-black geometric tiles, with the interiors designed by Paulo Lobo, who introduced two elegant spaces: a dining room (above) and open lounge/bar. In the middle is a curved, darkwood counter that wouldn't be out of place in a 1990s movie by Manoel de Oliveira (see p082). Offering refreshed Portuguese and European classics, the kitchen specialises in regional fish and seafood. The marinated mussels with lime and paprika is a good place to start, followed by the chargrilled tiger prawns on tagliolini — all the better washed down with a glass of Douro white. *Rua do Padrão 100, T 22 610 8059, www.cafeina.pt*

Taberna dos Mercadores

Many of the new wave *tabernas* pay lip service to Portuguese culinary traditions without actually imbuing much in the way of substance. But Taberna dos Mercadores, opened in 2014, does not scrimp on either quality or thrill. From an open kitchen comes perfectly cooked dorado, *açorda de mariscos* (the classic bread-based shellfish stew), pork ribs and Arouquesa veal, served to just a handful of tables. Suffused lighting, a nifty display of wine bottles tucked into the curved ceiling, and an abundance of lightwood create a cosy feel. The visual identity, from the menus mounted on pine to the matching blue-and-white chinaware, was created by Porto designers Raquel Rei and Ana Simões. The tavern is popular with those working in the local wine industry, so do book ahead.
Rua dos Mercadores 36-38, T 22 201 0510

Cantinho do Avillez

Chef José Avillez's Cantinho originated in Lisbon, and opened in Porto in 2014 (his restaurant Belcanto, also in the capital, holds two Michelin stars). The menu here delivers a fresh variation on home-style favourites: sautéed scallops served with trout eggs, crispy game sausage, and cod with breadcrumbs, for example. For this venture, there are also specialities, such as the Portuguesinha, a pie-based take on the *francesinha* (a classic Porto meat-stuffed sandwich that Scooby Doo would be proud of), to which Avillez adds truffle mortadella and truffle sauce. The informal but refined interior is by AnahoryAlmeida (see p097), who clad the walls in reclaimed wood and festooned them with retro kitchen items, from chopping boards to pepper mills.
Rua Mouzinho da Silveira 166,
T 22 322 7879, www.cantinhodoavillez.pt

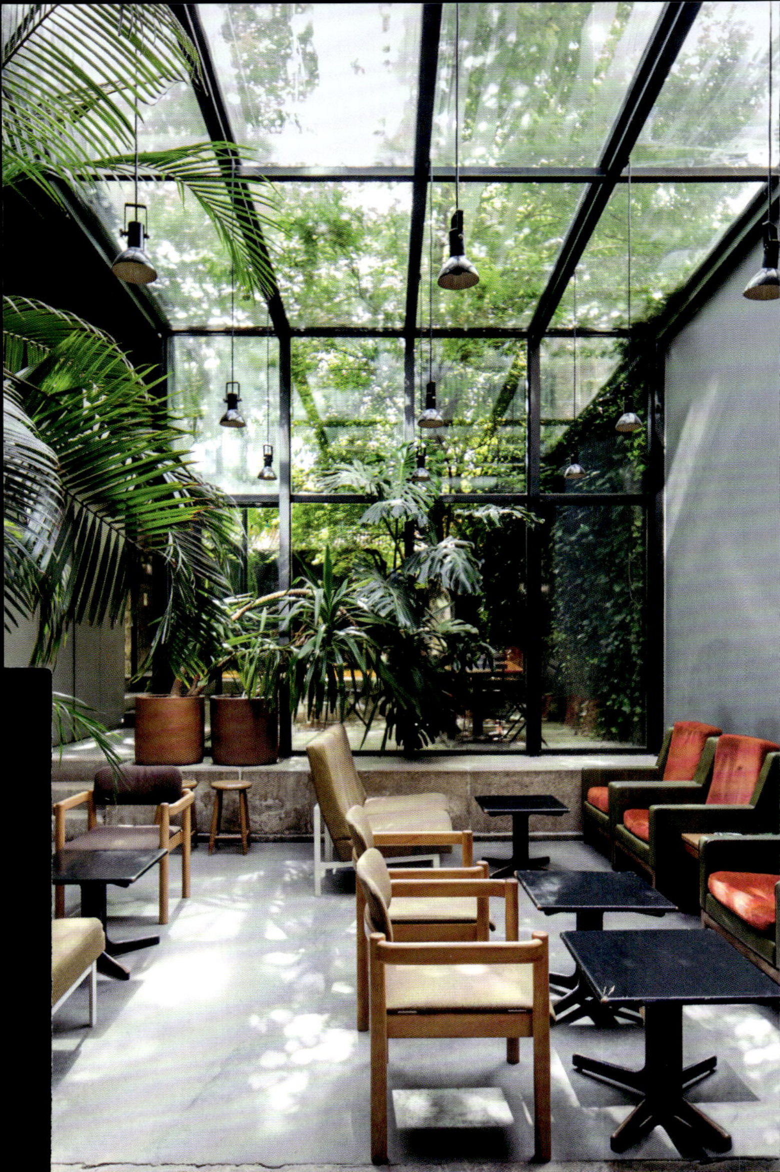

Café Vitória

This restaurant/café/bar (above) is a big favourite of the after-work crowd. When the weather is fine, do as the locals do and settle into one of the vintage chairs by the likes of António Garcia, José Espinho and Thonet in the courtyard or indoor garden (opposite) in the sleek glass-cube extension to this century-old building. Then order a top-quality cocktail or craft beer, ideally accompanied by *petiscos* (the Portuguese take on tapas), such as salt cod salad. The homey interior is by architect Miguel Tomé, who decorated it with pieces from Pedras & Pêssegos (see p064). Upstairs is a fine diner serving classic fare with a twist, like marinated sardines, swordfish ceviche and goat's cheese samosas, in a lovely setting featuring original wood panelling and tiles.
Rua José Falcão 156, T 22 013 5538, www.cafevitoria.com

Portucale

This extraordinary relic of pre-revolution decadence opened in 1969 on the top floor of the Miradouro apartment block. Many original features remain, from the building's tiled and panelled lobby to the bespoke cutlery on your table. Artist Guilherme Camarinha's fitted tapestries line the walls, somehow managing to meld futurism and Portuguese folklore. Likewise, the acclaimed food, overseen by Ernesto Azevedo's family, is a late-1960s take on national favourites — more modern palates may prefer the simpler dishes on the menu, like the grilled sea bass. Thanks to its position on a hill north-east of the centre, Portucale lays claim to the highest spot in the city, so the views are excellent. Make a reservation for just before sunset.
Rua da Alegria 598, T 22 537 0717, www.miradouro-portucale.com

Traça

Set in a restored 17th-century building, formerly a grocer, Traça serves classic Iberian comfort food, stylishly plated, and is best known for its excellent meat-led dishes. Two must-tries are the boar loin, breaded and stuffed with goat's cheese and foie, served on a spread of berry and apple puree; and the Charolais T-bone steak for two, which comes with salad and julienne fries. The open-plan, multi-level space has been warmly refurbished: the ceiling beams have been given a wash of white paint; antlers are mounted on walls; there are antique books, collected by the owners; and the pretty geometric tiling is an inspired touch. This is the perfect spot for a late supper on Fridays or Saturdays, when the atmosphere starts to get lively. *Largo de São Domingos 88, T 22 208 1065, www.restaurantetraca.com*

Casa d'Oro

Upon its completion in 1963, the Arrábida road bridge was the longest reinforced-concrete crossing in the world. Legendary civil engineer Edgar Cardoso oversaw its construction from a studio built to his own design and specifications in the bridge's shadow. Now known as the Casa d'Oro, the structure clings limpet-like to the river wall above the Douro, affording stunning views of Arrábida, the estuary and the Atlantic.

Since 2005, the 'House of Gold' has been home to an Italian eatery run by Maria Paola Porru, an Italian-born film-actress-turned-restaurateur. Her use of this Porto landmark respects the purity of Cardoso's semi-nautical, semi-cubist concept while also offering some superb cooking. In the summer, ask for a table on the terrace.
Rua do Ouro 797, T 22 610 6012,
www.restaurantecasanostra.com

Passos Manuel

This cinema/bar/disco is the handiwork of curator Pedro Gadanho, editor of the provocative architecture journal *Beyond*. Previously a screening room that was part of the Coliseu complex (see p076), Passos Manuel reopened in its own right in 2004. Porto's rising stars of music, art and design compete to stage events here — the kind of alternative and art house happenings that wouldn't get a look-in at the Coliseu.

The decor is modern yet also evokes the building's art deco heyday, with a mix of red neon, timber veneer and orange glass. Across the street is Maus Hábitos (T 22 208 7268), a multifaceted venue that comprises a vegetarian restaurant, a bar, a terrace and various exhibition spaces on the fourth floor of a garage that dates from the 1930s.
Rua de Passos Manuel 137, T 22 203 4121, www.passosmanuel.net

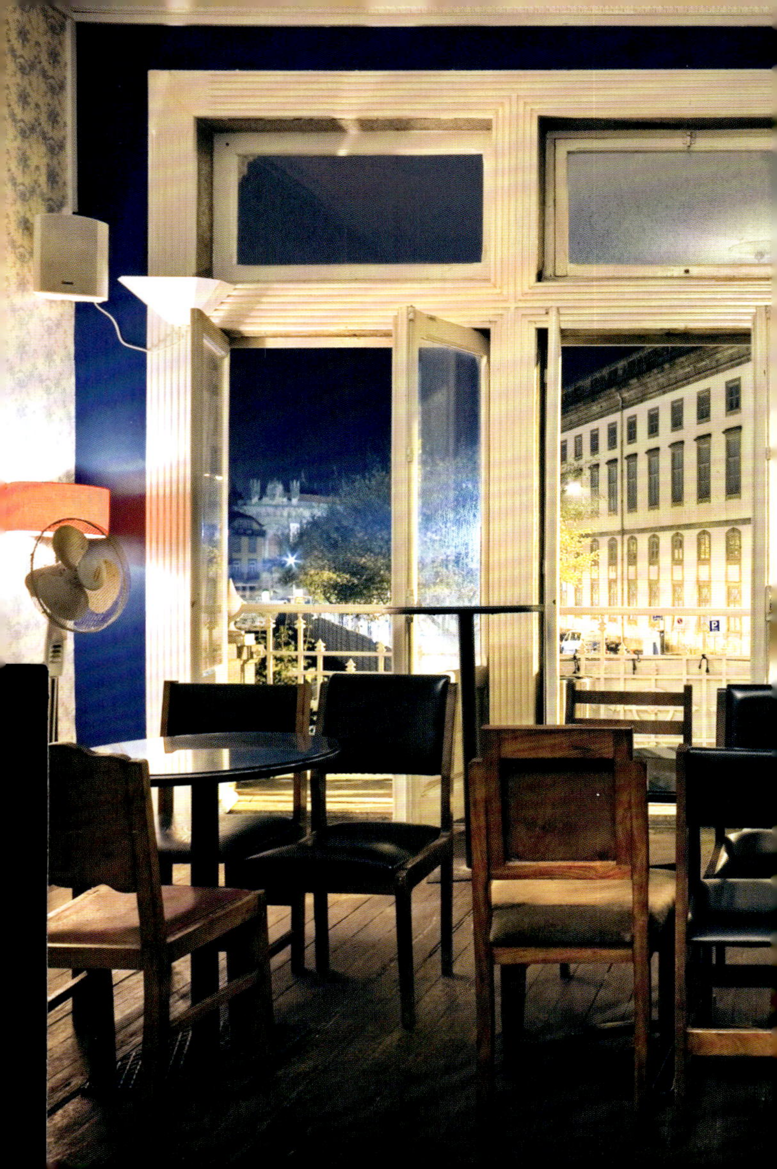

Era Uma Vez no Porto
A few doors away from Lello (see p095), 'Once Upon a Time in Porto' is a cosy first-floor bar in a converted apartment, with a balcony overlooking the Clérigos tower (see p009). Proprietors Nelson and Celia Pedrosa have created an edgy but sophisticated vibe, mixing eclectic 1950s furniture with chintzy wallpaper and a selection of work by on-the-rise artists.
Rua das Carmelitas 162, T 22 202 2240

Bop Café

Behind a gorgeous 1950s stone storefront with a retro light-bulb sign, this good-time café/bar displays a fantasy vinyl collection; around 3,000 records are shelved behind the counter, from jazz to pop, US folk and African rarities, collected by owners Filipe Ribeiro and João Brando. The fit-out, by designer Carlos Aguiar, riffs on the JBS jazz bar in Tokyo, and features pinewood cladding and listening posts – apart from the sheer excitement of sifting through the back catalogue, releases by local label Lovers & Lollypops are for sale. The all-day menu lists cereal and fruit in the morning, bagels for lunch, and comfort snacks, like mac and cheese, in the evening, when you should nab a seat at the bar to enjoy a few jars with Porto's bright young things.
Rua da Firmeza 575, T 22 200 1732, www.bop.pt

La Bohème Entre Amis

A buzzy coffee spot by day, La Bohème Entre Amis transforms into a sleek bar in the evenings. Set on Rua Galeria de Paris, it is distinctive for its granite facade and wood-and-glass canopy, which draws you inside. It's a quite natural extension of the interior, by architects Atelier Veloso, who have installed a comprehensive ribbed pinewood framework that unifies the airy three-level establishment. All that timber is complemented by simple black-leather upholstered seating, and the many bottles on display. Indeed, the wine list is rather special and exclusively Portuguese, with labels from the Douro to the Algarve. Soak it up with tapas. We're fans of the Pica-pau, which here is a deconstructed *francesinha* sandwich presented as a sharing plate.
Rua Galeria de Paris 40, T 22 201 5154, www.laboheme.com.pt

Café Ceuta

Once all the hip bars currently setting up around the centre of town have retired their dancing shoes, we like to think that the institution that is Café Ceuta will still be serving quality cups of joe and providing another generation of students and yet-to-be-discovered authors with free wi-fi. A much-loved piece of history from 1953, Ceuta is a terrazzo-lined coffee house and restaurant at ground level (above) with a spacious billiard and games hall below, unchanged since the day it opened – it is the only one of Porto's major cafés to have survived intact. The staff are wonderfully attentive, and the clientele fiercely loyal as a result. It has also preserved a sense of postwar optimism that gladdens the soul, making it the after-hours hangout of choice for discerning Portuenses. Closed Sundays.
Rua de Ceuta 20, T 22 200 9376

Café Candelabro

Ever since the jeunesse dorée rediscovered Downtown, just about every shop here is beginning to look as if it is a nightclub-in-waiting. Although the instinct of many a local entrepreneur is to gut these spaces and start again, a different approach was taken at Café Candelabro – a beautifully reworked bar that attracts a sophisticated but informal clientele. Occupying a former bookstore that had been here since the 1950s, the venture, which opened in 2009, is run by cousins Miguel Seabra and Hugo Brito. Working with architect António Pedro Valente, they maximised the character of the interior – especially the attractive tiled floor – while maintaining a modern edge. Head over for afternoon coffee, or a white port with tonic and the cheeseboard.
Rua da Conçeicão 3,
www.cafecandelabro.com

INSIDER'S GUIDE
ESTELITA MENDONÇA, FASHION DESIGNER

Porto born and bred and a graduate of the city's Fashion Academy, Estelita Mendonça established his eponymous label in 2010. He describes his home town as 'curious, a bit dark, a bit melancholy, it's a very special place'. Over the last decade or so he has witnessed the city transform from a sleepy port to a much more cosmopolitan destination. 'That contrast really appeals to me, and this mix of people and stories is a major influence on my work.'

A typical day is spent working in his studio, but it is conveniently located near versatile Maus Hábitos (see p047), where, according to Mendonça, you can have it all: 'See an exhibition, order a pizza, have a coffee with friends, and even go clubbing.' Also around the corner is Mundano Objectos (see p061). 'It's my favourite store as there's a beautifully curated selection of furniture and objects.' For under-the-radar exploring, he recommends Espaço Mira (Rua de Miraflor 159, T 929 145 191) for photo exhibitions, and Nova Sintra Park (Rua de Barão da Nova Sintra) for its historic fountains.

Mendonça is also a stylist and DJ, so he is often out on the town. Cometa (Rua de Tomás Gonzaga 87, T 916 582 608) is his pick for dinner: 'They do the best steak tartare.' Later, you might find him at Passos Manuel (see p047), the multi-room club Plano B (Rua de Cândido dos Reis 30) or, in the early hours, in the tunnel-shaped techno temple Gare (Rua da Madeira 182, T 914 604 377).
For full addresses, see Resources.

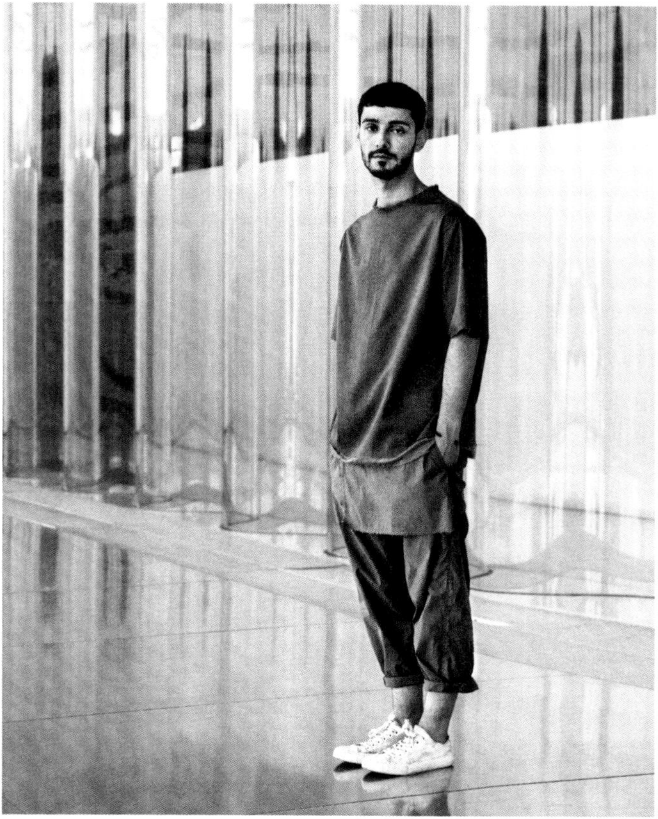

ART AND DESIGN
GALLERIES, STUDIOS AND PUBLIC SPACES

Though Lisboetas would never admit it, Portugal's second city has always been more proactive creatively, partly because cheaper rents and production costs have attracted emerging talent from the fields of fashion to furniture. Indeed, some of the capital's best art spaces originated here, like Múrias Centeno (see p058), Ó! Galeria (see p060) and Quadrado Azul (see p066). They cluster in 'Bombarda', a scene kick-started when Fernando Santos (see p062) opened in 1993 in this once quiet residential enclave, which now has more than 20 galleries, a slew of design stores and hip event spaces/bars such as Breyner85 (Rua do Breiner 85, T 22 201 3172); *inaugurações simultâneas* take place on bi-monthly Saturdays. For a superlative overview of contemporary Portuguese art, do not miss Serralves (see p068). It has more than 4,300 works, the main body of which begins 'Circa 1968' (the title of its opening exhibition), through the post-1974 flowering of artistic freedom, right up to the present day.

Porto's history as a place of makers, for everything from wine to shoes, has held it in good stead in terms of design. Seek out the handmade wooden furniture by Piurra (Rua do Rosário 147, T 913 468 263) and Made In* (see p064), and the edit of local pieces at Mundano Objectos (see p061). Graphic design is also highly valued. In 2014, White Studio refreshed the city's visual identity with a cute riff on its azulejos, adding to its unique legacy of tile art (opposite). *For full addresses, see Resources.*

Quem es, Porto?

Any visitor to Porto will admire the azulejo tiles adorning its buildings, especially the elaborate friezes, like those at São Bento station (see p072). From the early 1950s, a cohort of ceramicists in Lisbon adopted a functionalist approach to the art form; one of the central figures was Maria Keil, whose vibrant 1980s murals spruce up Lisbon's metro stations. Porto-based Júlio Resende (see p077) was very active in the scene; our favourite work is his painterly 1987 *Ribeira Negra*, which spans a wall near Ponte Luís I and depicts tableaux from daily life. A new wave of creatives has adopted the glazed stoneware as a canvas. The collaborative project *Quem es, Porto?* ('Who Are You, Porto?'), installed in 2015 on a facade in the centre of town, comprises a mosaic of 3,000 tiles each hand-painted by a local. *Rua da Madeira*

Múrias Centeno
Since 2007, gallerist Nuno Centeno has been influential in the Porto scene, along with ventures including the artist-run A Certain Lack of Coherence (T 919 272 115). In 2014, he banded together with Bruno Múrias and also launched in Lisbon. On an exciting roster now are locals Carla Filipe, whose drawings and texts present streams of consciousness; performance artist and technology pioneer Silvestre Pestana; and Mauro Cerqueira, who channels social comment through multidisciplinary means. Represented too are global artists, many from Brazil, including F Marquespenteado ('Sujeitos Desconhecidos Melo A Vasos Solitários', above). Shows take place in a long room that stretches deep behind the glass facade, and a small space at the rear.
Rua Miguel Bombarda 531, T 936 866 492, www.muriascenteno.com

ART/DESIGN

Ó! Galeria

This informal, relentlessly cheerful spot is a little different to its sparsely designed, more serious neighbours in the gallery district. It focuses on illustration, drawing and publishing, and can be counted on for a consistent variety of colourful one-off pieces and prints featuring bold statements and offbeat characters. Since opening in 2009, it has exhibited work by talent from right across the globe, including Argentine Maria Luque, France's Virginie Morgand and Pole Karol Banach, and also has a fine collection of original 'zines and books. Well-known Lisbon muralist Tamara Alves is a regular collaborator. Owner Ema Ribeiro's mission to enhance the pubic perception of illustration as an art form seems to be working – Ó! has now launched in Lisbon.

Rua Miguel Bombarda 61, T 930 558 047, www.ogaleria.com

Mundano Objectos

Sofia Assalino and Luis Cavalheiro's bijou concept store is packed with a well-edited selection of far-from-mundane objects for practically every part of your house, even down to books, art, fragrances, fashion and an organic deli. It is mostly the global design names on sale, from the Campana brothers to Inga Sempé, Naoki Terada and Hella Jongerius, and there are plenty of Scandi brands – we spied HAY's 'Uchiwa' lounge chair and Bolia's concrete 'Cemento' bowls. But do look out for the local items, such as wooden furniture by Mo-ow, Fiu's 'hanging gardens', eco-friendly stools by Ply&Co, and Galula's playful lighting. Such is Mundano's depth of interest that you may well go in for a pair of stylish bookends only to emerge with a pair of AIAIAI earbuds.
Rua de Santos Pousada 668, T 916 352 335, www.mundanopt

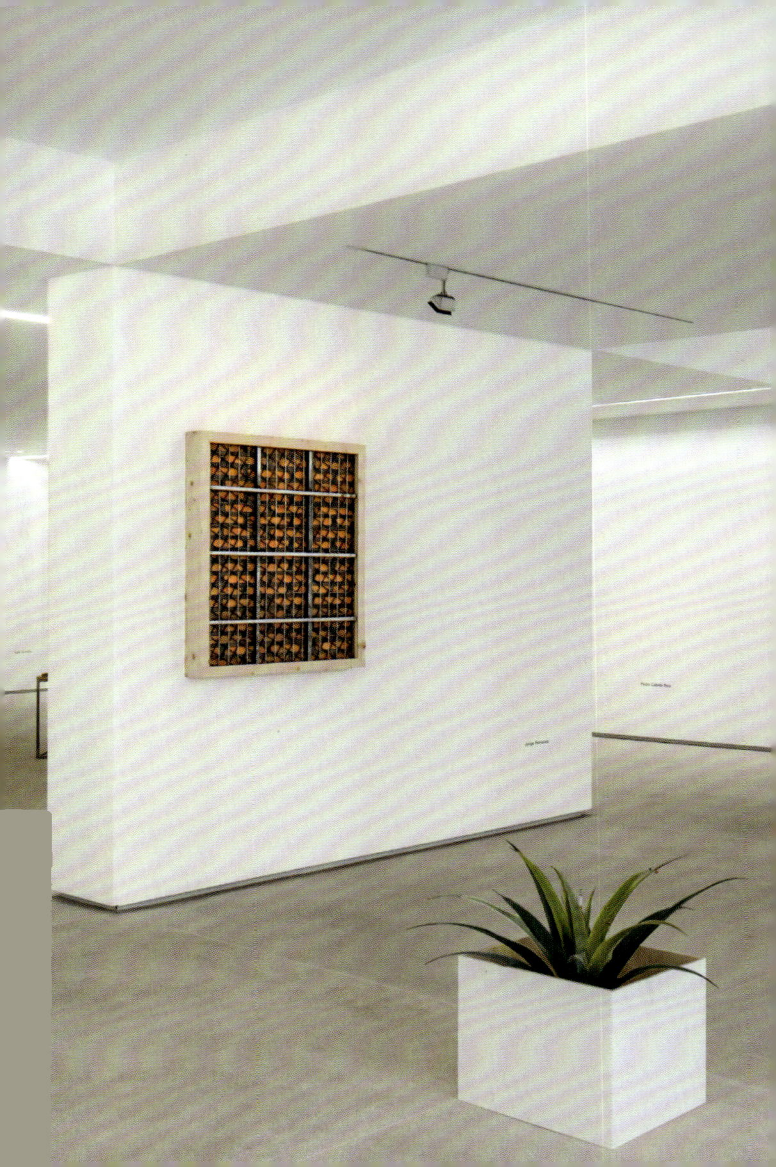

Galeria Fernando Santos
A forerunner of the Rua Miguel Bombarda scene, Fernando Santos has been putting on consistently impressive shows for a quarter of a century and is a ground zero for local collectors. It represents around 40 strong names, both international and Portuguese – among these, Pedro Cabrita Reis, Pedro Calapez, Gerardo Burmester (*Untitled*; pictured, right) and Bosco Sodi.
Rua Miguel Bombarda 526, T 22 606 1090

ART/DESIGN

Pedras & Pêssegos

This sprawling whitewashed warehouse, once a printer's, is a great place to browse, due to its diverse collection of midcentury design, art and antiques. It specialises in Danish furniture from the 1940s to 1970s: classics all, from names like Hans J Wegner, Alvar Aalto, Finn Juhl, Arne Jacobsen and Børge Mogensen. Also on Rua do Almada, Casa Almada (No 544, T 919 893 040) has a similar abundance of vintage pieces and affinity to Scandinavia, in a restored piano-repair workshop – a series of pared-down granite rooms linked by a beautiful timber ceiling. Open 2-7pm Tuesday to Friday and 11am-1pm and 3-7pm on Saturday. Further down the road, Casa Almada's follow-up, Made In* (No 331), is a collaboration with Miguel Cunha, Pedro e Ines and Susana Beirão, showcasing contemporary work.
Rua do Almada 558, T 915 907 723

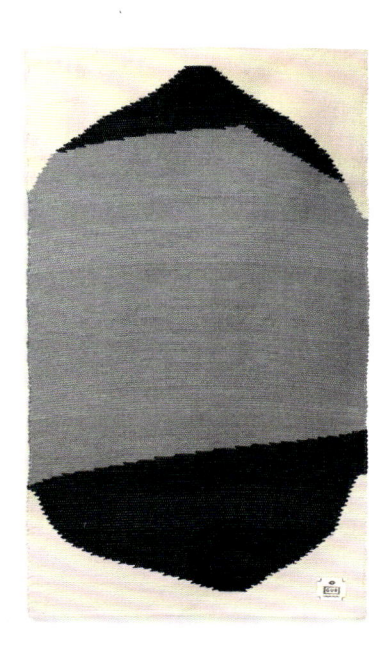

Gur
Célia Esteves established Gur in 2013, and produces limited-edition rugs, which also function as wall hangings, in collaboration with artists and design firms around the world; an early collection was made with Bombarda drawing gallery Dama Aflita (see p020). Using artisan techniques, the pieces are made from recycled cotton *tirela* (rags) and handwoven on looms in Viana do Castelo, in northern Portugal.

This process informs Esteves' philosophy of creating modest, authentic objects with a modern aesthetic. 'An Attempt to Occupy' (above), €100, forms part of a series of 12 made in partnership with Italian brand Fabrica Features and its stable of young creatives – the simple, abstract shape was dreamed up by Tomoni Maezawa. Browse others at Coração Alecrim (T 938 111 152).
T 912 307 453, www.rugbygur.com

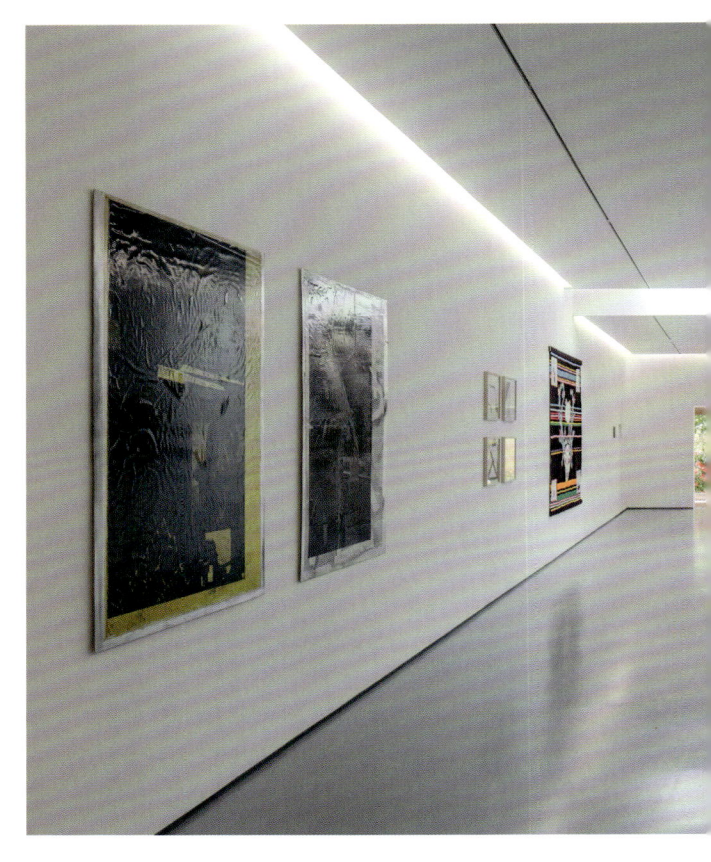

Galeria Quadrado Azul

A pioneering gallery established in 1986, Quadrado Azul preceded even Serralves (overleaf) and was the first venue in the country to show work by Salvador Dalí. Founded by the collector Manuel Ulisses, its name ('Blue Square') is inspired by the futuristic work *K4*, a satirical pamphlet by the Lisbon agitator and multidisciplinary artist Almada Negreiros written in 1917. Besides representing names like Álvaro Lapa, Francisco Tropa and Nadir Afonso, often in group shows ('Untitled', above), the enterprise supports students from the Porto School of Fine Arts. It joined the Rua Miguel Bombarda crowd in the noughties, organising its space into five 'moments' (entrance, nave, skylight, exit, courtyard), executed by architects Brandão Costa.
Rua Miguel Bombarda 553, T 22 609 7313, www.quadradoazul.pt

ART/DESIGN

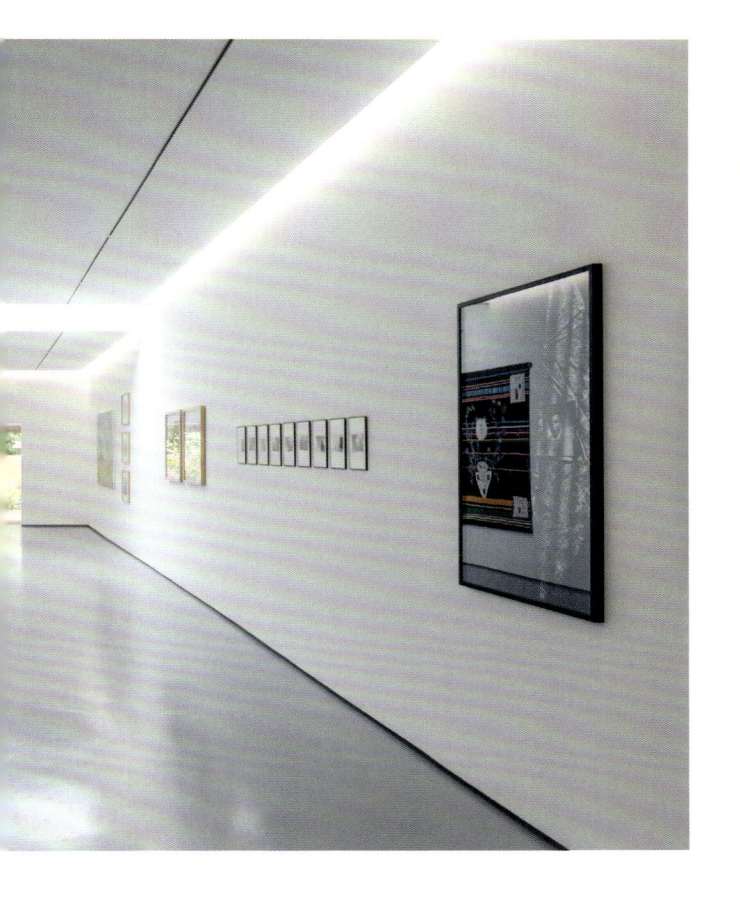

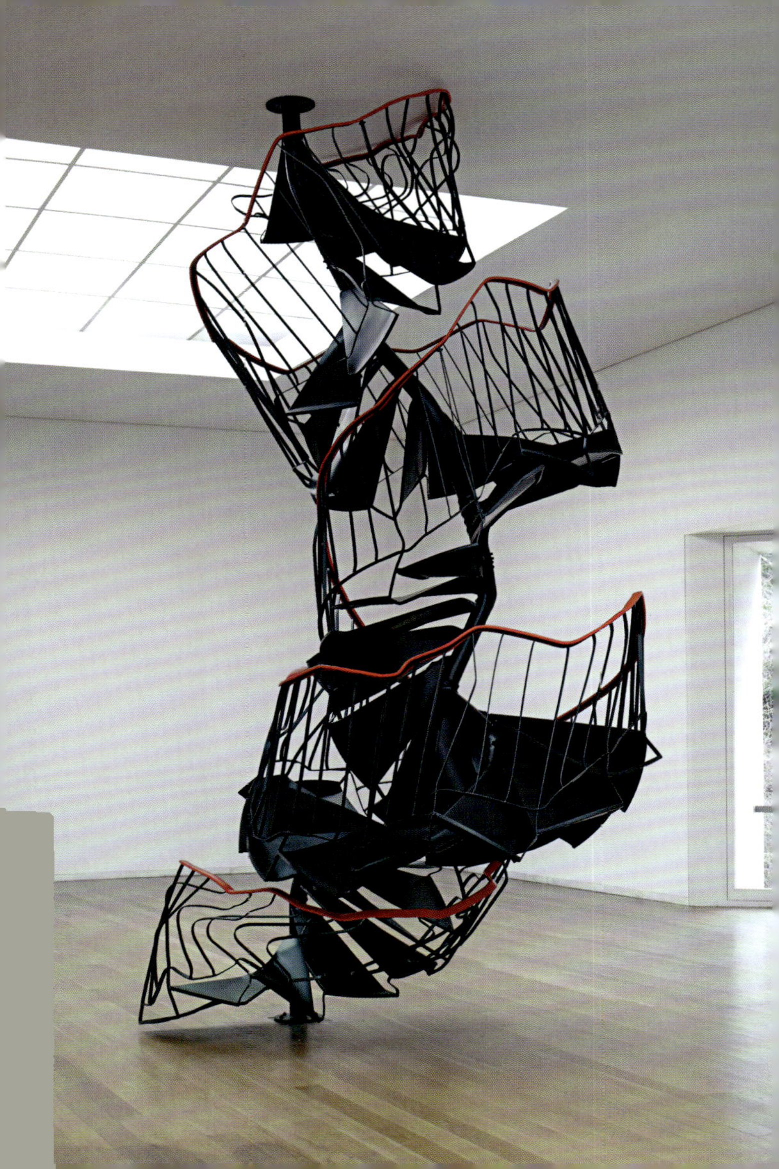

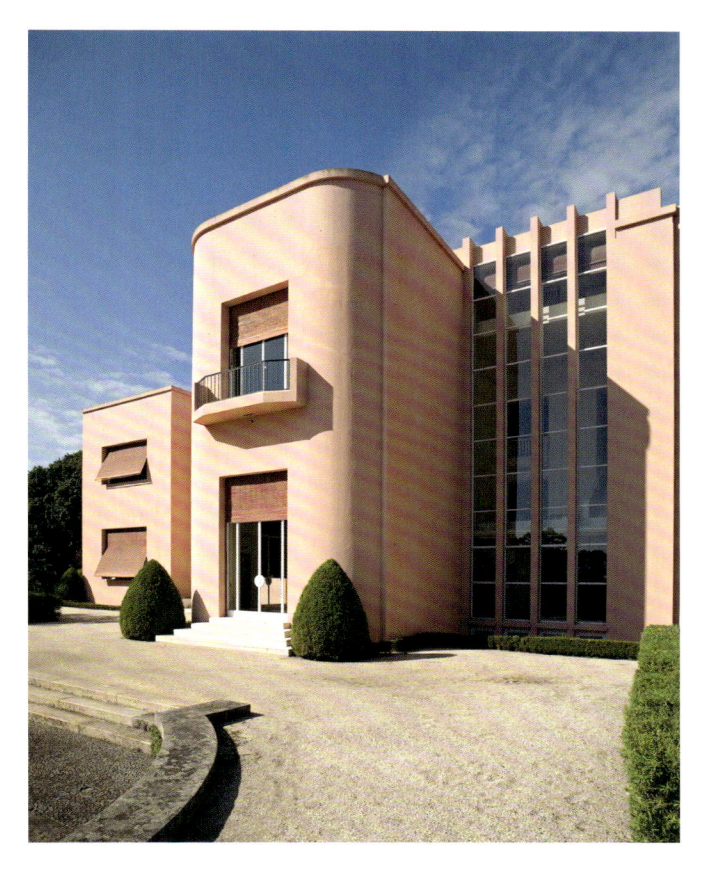

Fundação de Serralves
Not only is this one of the best collections of contemporary art in Portugal, but the estate is worth visiting for its architecture alone. The 1925 mansion (above) is an art deco delight by José Marques da Silva, with a René Lalique skylight, and a neo-baroque chapel that is completely enveloped within the pink walls. The landscaping is proto-modernism at its most flamboyant. The museum, which often features large-scale installations such as Monika Sosnowska's 'Architectonisation' (opposite), and library, with a Tobias Rehberger ceiling installation, occupy a substantial 1999 building by Siza Vieira — a sculptural white box in tune with its setting. The top-floor restaurant here offers an exceptional lunch buffet, which should be taken on the roof on warm days.
Rua de Dom João de Castro 210,
T 22 615 6500, www.serralves.pt

Kubik Gallery
Located in Cais das Pedra, on the river, west of the old customs house, Kubik emerged in 2010 as a space to promote 'originality'. It puts on two-monthly exhibitions by up-and-coming artists, mainly from Europe (local boy Pedro Tudela's 'Outro'; pictured). There's also an exterior 4 sq m cubicle with a glass door displaying guerilla interventions.
Rua da Restauração 6, T 22 600 4927

ART/DESIGN

ARCHITOUR
A GUIDE TO PORTO'S ICONIC BUILDINGS

Porto is famed for its modernism, largely due to the country's best-known living architect, Siza Vieira. His oeuvre ranges from an early domestic refurb that houses Casa da Arquitectura (Rua Roberto Ivens 582, T 22 240 4663) to progressive social housing at Bouça (see p074) and the geometric tricks of Faculdade de Arquitectura (see p084). His mentor, Fernando Távora, one of the fathers of the Porto School, rejuvenated Palácio do Freixo (see p023) on the city's outskirts late in his career. His best central project is the tennis pavilion at Quinta da Conceição (Avenida Dr Antunes Guimarães). Another alumnus, Eduardo Souto de Moura, gifted Porto both the Torre Burgo (see p012) and Casa do Cinema (see p082).

Earlier architecture includes the work of José Marques da Silva, whose 1916 Beaux Arts São Bento station (Praça de Almeida Garrett) has a ticket hall by George Colaço with 550 sq m of azulejo tiles, the art deco Coliseu (see p076), and Artur Andrade's virtuoso Cinema Batalha (Praça da Batalha 47), an expressive piece of modernism from 1947 wrapped around a 1908 structure, with agitprop reliefs. Sadly, it is forlorn and neglected, yet its legacy lives on, as local practices hark back to this more playful era, notably Barbosa & Guimarães, whose Vodafone HQ (Avenida da Boavista 2949) has a crystalline form and fine concrete detailing, and Luís Pedro Silva, with a cruise terminal (opposite) that seems to slowly unravel.
For full addresses, see Resources.

Terminal de Cruzeiros

The glinting 2015 cruise ship terminal in the port of Leixões, once a hub of the local fishing and canning industries, is a marker of how Porto's economy is refocusing. The facility accommodates liners up to 300m long and encompasses a marina for 170 vessels. Luís Pedro Silva's building might well be white, following Siza Vieira's great lead, but it differs in its sinuous curves that spin passengers around a bend in the jetty, delivering them out to sea or back to shore. Spiralling ramps envelop the structure like a lazily spooled ribbon, linking functions, guiding circulation and heading up to a rooftop auditorium. The facade too is a local tribute – ceramic tiles – but with a twist, literally, as the hexagonal blocks are angled and rotated, evoking barnacles, and reflect the sunlight in myriad directions.
Avenida Comércio de Leixões, www.apdl.pt

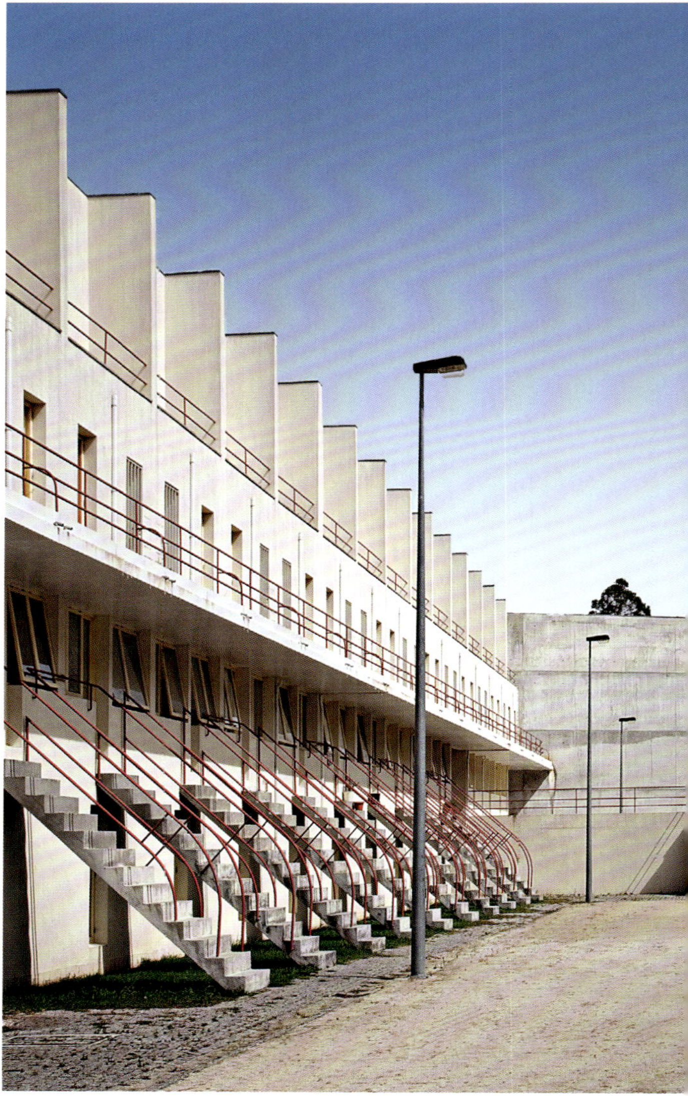

Bairro da Bouça
After the military coup in 1974, a group of designers formed SAAL, in order to provide decent central accommodation for the working class. Bouça is an estate of 128 townhouses united by a concrete wall that forms three elongated plazas. Not totally finished until 2006, it is now popular with well-heeled buyers seeking a slice of Siza Vieira in a prime location.
Rua da Boavista/Rua das Águas Férreas

Coliseu

A landmark of late art deco with a neon-clad tower, the Coliseu was designed by a team of architects led by Cassiano Branco, and opened in 1941. It houses a 3,000-seat concert hall with sweeping galleries, a 300-capacity 'attic' room and the cinema/bar Passos Manuel (see p047). Everything was custom-made, from the wall reliefs to the light fittings, doors, windows, chandeliers and commissioned paintings, and the foyer appears untouched since its heyday despite the fact that the building has weathered neglect and a fire, and was almost sold in 1995; it was preserved as a venue only after mass public demonstrations. Another sign of Porto's formidable people power is that it is the cheap seats (*balcão popular*) here that are said to enjoy the best acoustics.
Rua de Passos Manuel 137, T 22 339 4940, www.coliseu.pt

Igreja de Nossa Senhora da Boavista
The work of architect Agostinho Ricca has been rather overshadowed by the stellar careers of Siza Vieira, Távora and Souto de Moura, but Ricca also played a major role in the evolution of the 20th-century city. From the early 1960s and right through the 1970s, he worked on an estate in Boavista, which references Alvar Aalto, Frank Lloyd Wright and Carlo Scarpa. But it was Denys Lasdun who had arguably the greatest influence on this brutalist concrete-and-glass church, built between 1977 and 1981, at the centre of the development. As at Lasdun's National Theatre in London, it displays the timber framework into which the concrete was poured. It is made up of perpendicular strata (overleaf), and has a stained-glass window by Júlio Resende.
Rua Azevedo Coutinho 103, T 22 600 2691, www.paroquia-boavista.org

Igreja de Nossa Senhora da Boavista

ARCHITOUR

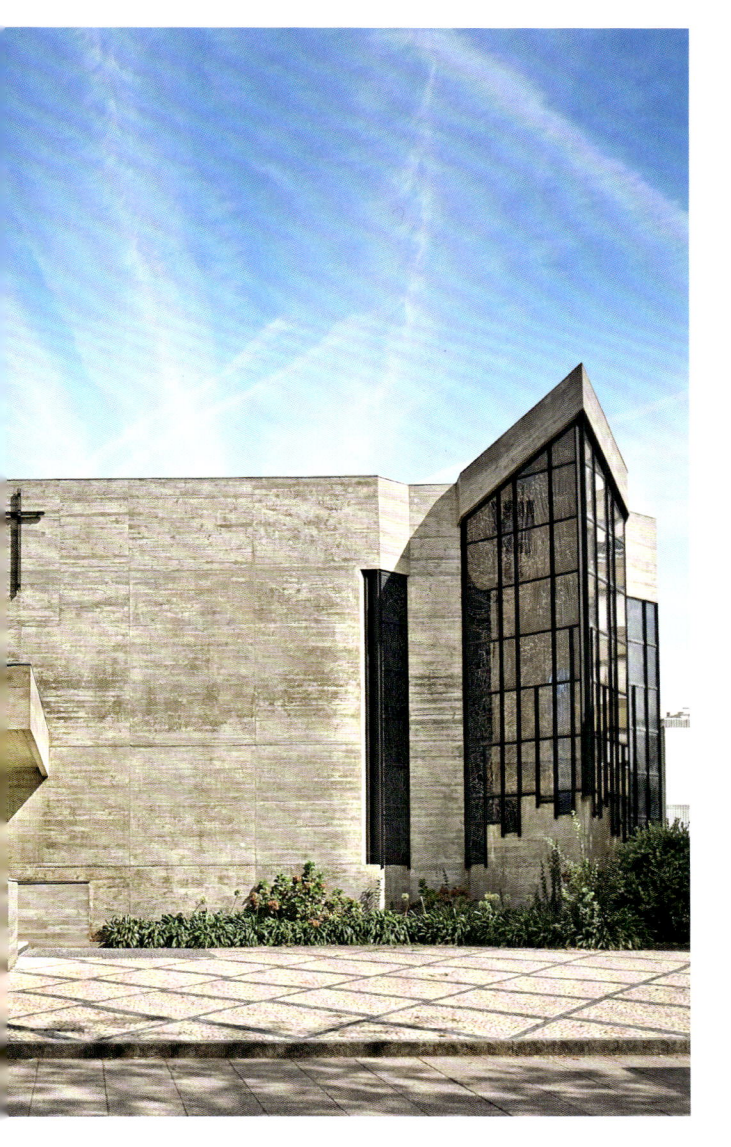

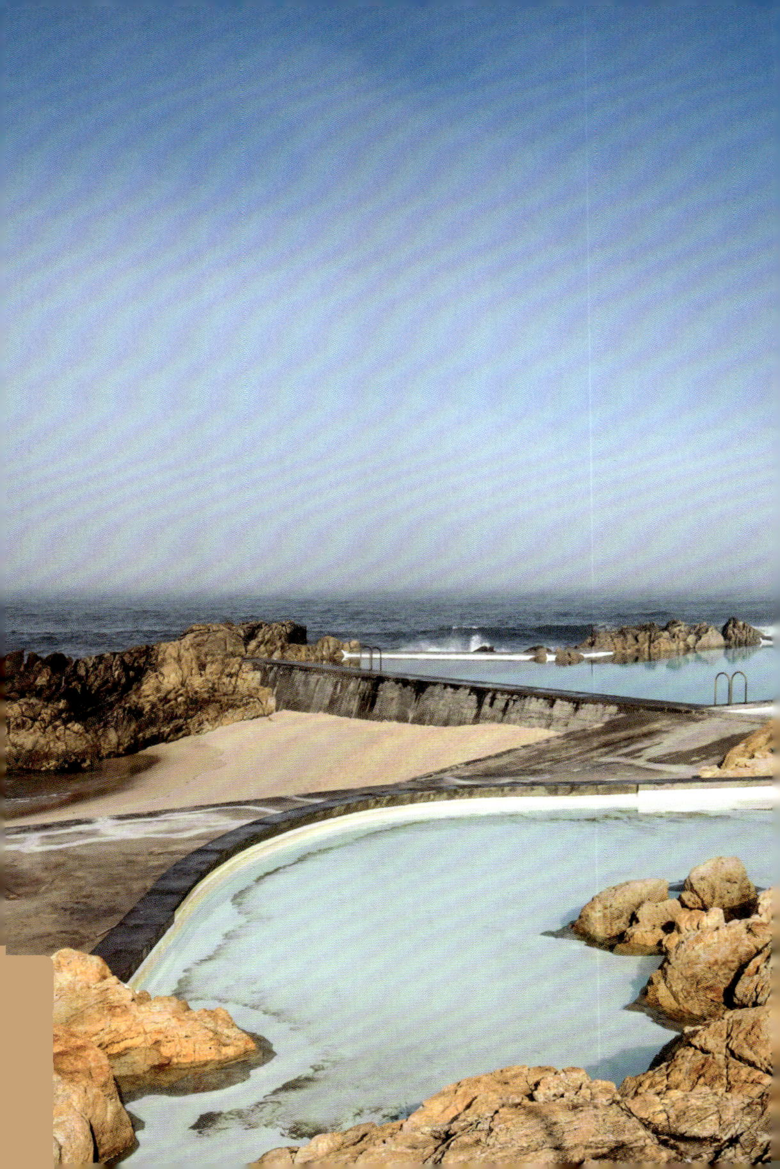

Piscina das Marés

One of Siza Vieira's earliest works, which brought him global attention, the 'Pool of Tides' is a profound piece of landscape design on the rocky seafront of Leça da Palmeira, close to his virtuoso Boa Nova teahouse (see p027), also from the early 1960s. From the coastal road, you descend into dark, dramatic changing rooms and emerge to a vista over the granite coast. The swimming areas are artfully carved out of the rocks and supported by concrete walls, allowing bathing in what would be an otherwise inhospitable landscape. There is also a very elegantly composed café and terrace. The unheated pools are open in the summer only and have an eerie feel in the colder months. Since it was unveiled in 1966, the ensemble has inspired architects including Peter Zumthor and Zaha Hadid.
Avenida da Liberdade, T 22 995 2610

Casa do Cinema Manoel de Oliveira

This quirky structure, defined by two big, periscope-like windows, is Souto de Moura at his most expressive. It wryly pretends to be similar to the surrounding houses in this unassuming neighbourhood in Foz, and the distorted volume (it is a trapezoid shape when seen from above) adapts to the small plots characteristic of the locale. It was intended to house the work of film auteur Manoel de Oliveira – hence the lens effect – but a long-running dispute meant it did not come to be and the 2003 building has never opened to the public. However, since Oliveira's death in 2015, there has been energetic debate about its use and a renewed interest in turning it into a bona fide cultural venue. In the meantime, the exterior is worth the trip alone, although be ready to tackle security to get near it.
Rua Bartolomeu Velho

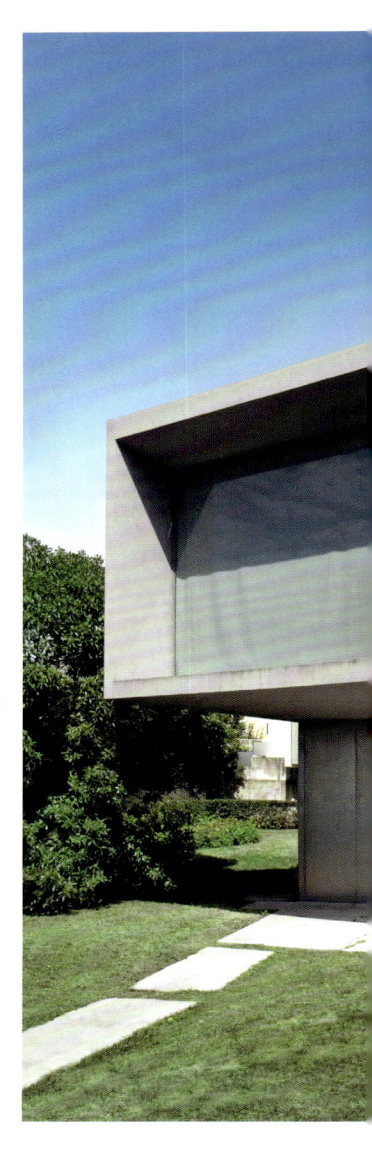

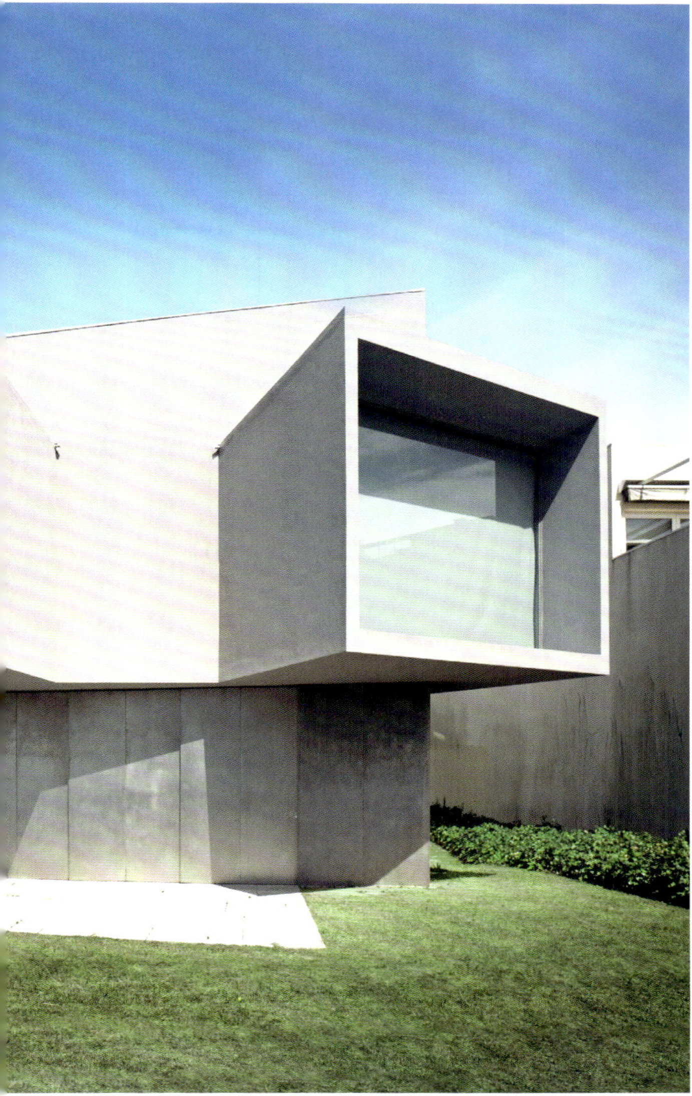

Faculdade de Arquitectura
The Porto School emerged in the 1950s as university professors Carlos Ramos and Fernando Távora looked for ways to marry the dictats of modernism with a regional sensibility. After studying here, Siza Vieira followed this approach and would later develop a style that combined high-quality materials, site-generated geometries and white-rendered forms. He came back to teach at the architecture faculty in spells from 1966, and, naturally enough, was the only choice to overhaul and modernise the campus. Completed in 1994 on a difficult plot – triangular and sloping – he devised a series of pavilions on terraces with the circulation positioned underground. It is an excellent example of his style. Also seek out his mid-1980s Carlos Ramos Pavilion, an elegant block at the back of the site.
Via Panorâmica, T 22 605 7100

Pavilhão Rosa Mota

Built in 1953 and originally named, simply, the Sports Pavilion, this ambitous project by José Carlos Loureiro is distinguished by its copper-clad reinforced concrete dome, lined with hundreds of circular skylights. It is a grand modernist gesture within the historic landscaped gardens designed by the German Émile David, although many locals preferred the 1865 Joseph Paxton-inspired Palácio de Cristal exhibition hall it replaced. It was renamed Rosa Mota after the local hero and first Portuguese woman to win an Olympic gold medal, in the marathon at Seoul 1988, but the arena has never lived up to this bestowal, and is now mostly used by school teams, and for trade fairs and exhibitions. However, it is being refurbished and extended for 2020, in the hope of inspiring future generations.
Rua Dom Manuel II, T 22 543 0360

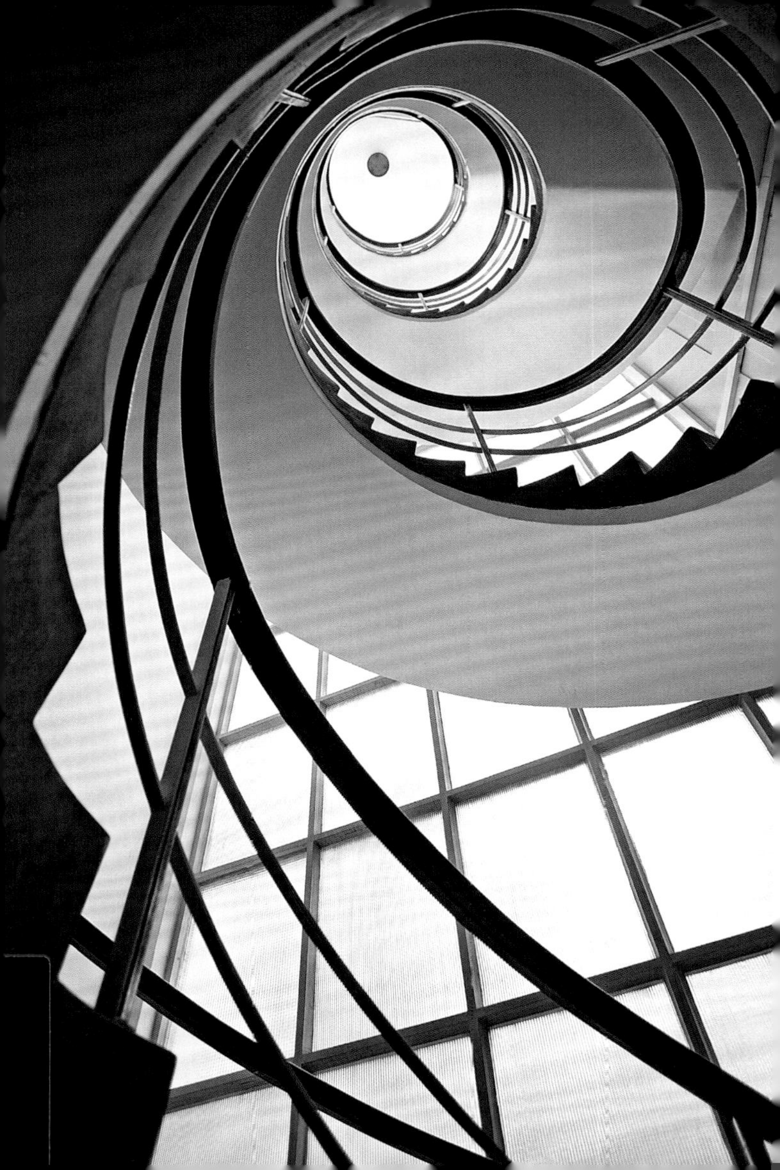

Edifício Soares & Irmão

In the early 1940s, Arménio Losa was part of a coterie of architects who proposed a road connecting Avenida dos Aliados with the Palácio de Cristal (see p085). It was thwarted by a huge lump of granite, which proved too costly to move, and the steeply inclined Rua de Ceuta remains as a slice of an unfulfilled urban plan. It is flanked by several Athens Charter-era buildings, including this one for the Soares & Irmão company, designed in 1953 by Losa and his partner Cassiano Barbosa. The Corbusian facade, held on the perpendicular by piloti, is defined by the confident brise-soleil with mobile louvres. Inside, a quite beautiful spiral staircase (opposite), reminiscent of Erich Mendelsohn at his finest, runs up a light well. The building now serves as the offices of Luís Pedro Silva (see p073).
Rua de Ceuta 16

SHOPS
THE BEST RETAIL THERAPY AND WHAT TO BUY

During the noughties, the centre of the city appeared to be doomed as a retail destination, with shoppers instead heading to suburban megamalls. Perhaps because of this exodus, it has retained a large number of characterful businesses still in their original premises. Of particular note are the labyrinthine hardware shops along Rua do Almada, which is known as the 'street of machines'. There are also some excellent vintage furniture warehouses (see p064).

The Bombarda area (see p056) throws up no end of delights for the casual browser, from galleries to design brands, organic grocers and tea salons. And Porto's menswear scene is hugely impressive, headed up by La Paz (see p092). New wave talent is found in the concept stores: look for Hugo Costa at Daily Day (see p090) and Pedro Pedro at Scar-ID (Rua do Rosário 253, T 22 203 3087), where ladies are catered for by local fashion designer Ana Segurado.

The city is, of course, synonymous with port, which is produced in the Douro Valley. Skip touristy Gaia for tastings in the Jardins do Palácio de Cristal at Antiqvvm (Rua de Entre Quintas 220, T 22 600 0445), and purchase your chosen label from Cleriporto (Rua da Assunção 38, T 22 203 8027). Foodies should head to the delis in and around the 19th-century Mercado do Bolhão (Rua Formosa). Perhaps pick up some artisan cheeses – Rabaçal (hard) or Serra da Estrela (soft) – to complete the after-dinner experience.

For full addresses, see Resources.

Say My Name

An alumnus and now professor at Porto's Gudi school of fashion, Catarina Sequeira established her womenswear label, Say My Name, in 2007, and the brand has since flourished in Portugal, as well as across East Asia. A flagship store opened in 2015 within a 1970s cinema-turned-mall, and was designed by local firm Ding Dong. It sports a monochrome palette combined with futuristic aspects, such as a screen of alternating black metal and mirrored panelling. The garments meld refined tailoring with edgy details – a pencil skirt is embellished with frou-frou elements like ruffles, and knitwear is playfully tufted and oversized, for example – and hang from a fluid railing. Look out for Lisbon-based Daniela Catraia's line of shoes and bags.
Loja 7, Galerias Lumière, Rua José Falcão 157, T 932 479 184, www.saymyname.pt

Daily Day
Opened in 2015, this happening concept store does a terrific job of championing prêt-à-porter from the region and beyond, with a well-judged blend of homegrown product and garments, such as spectacles by Paulino, Lobo Marinho pocket squares, and soft shirts from Portuguese Flannel (whose aesthetic is more Portland than Porto), as well as select pieces by Say My Name (see p089). Daily Day's in-house line of mens- and womenswear is created by Vânia Villas Boas, whose relaxed designs promote cool functionality over trends; boxy-cut denim dresses and loose-fitting colour-blocked T-shirts, for instance. The shop operates as something of a cultural hub, hosting events like poetry readings, exhibits and low-key pop performances.
Praça General Humberto Delgado 263, T 22 319 4583, www.daily-day.com

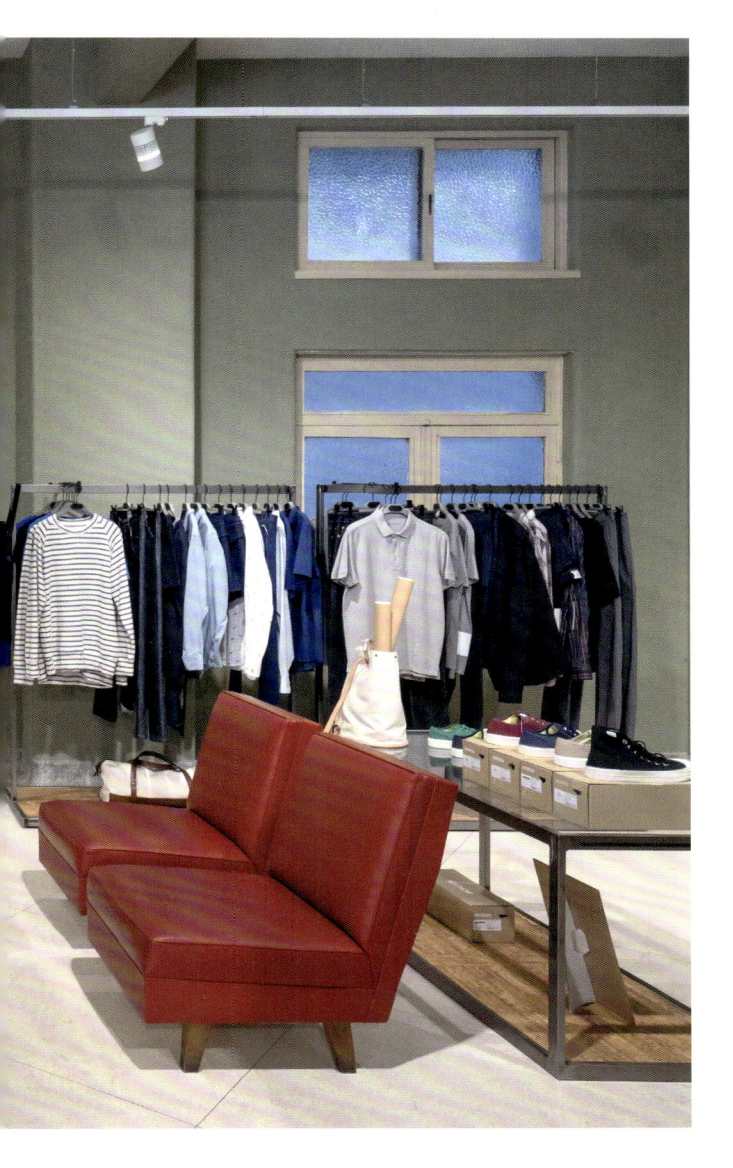

SHOPS

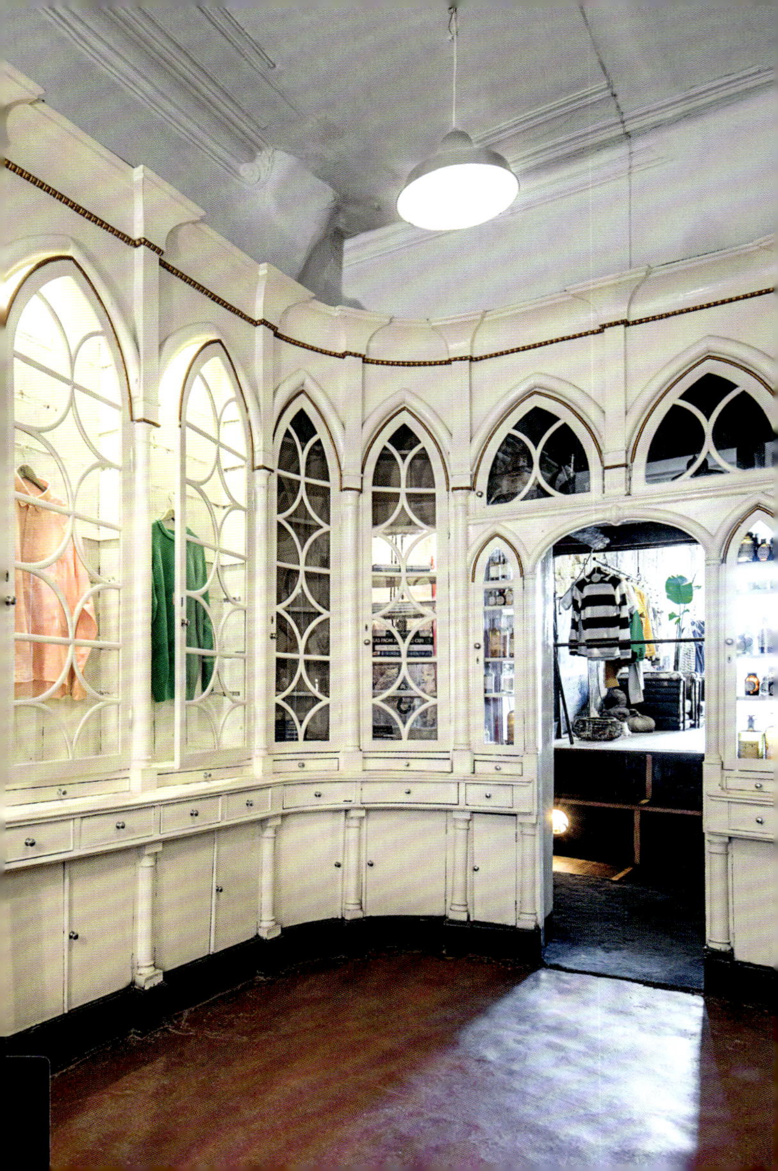

La Paz

This seriously stylish menswear label was launched in 2011 by André Bastos Teixeira and José Miguel Abreu. The ethos is classic silhouettes with thoughtful craftsmanship, underlined by a nifty maritime aesthetic. The handsome, if somewhat haphazard flagship is set inside a former pharmacy that was popular with sailors arriving at the old docks, and many of the original features have been retained, such as the bijou cabinetry, with small interventions by architects Skrei. The brand puts a strong emphasis on local production; stock up on the natty socks, woven on Madeira island. We also fell for the fisherman's jumpers, and the cotton 'Alegre' shirt (above), €125, patterned with boats. Wear it back home to conjure up sun-bleached days by the sea. *Rua da Reboleira 23, T 22 202 5037, www.lapaz.pt*

Wrong Weather

Impressive not only for its deconstructivist, angled layout, which borrows heavily from the nearby Vodafone HQ (see p072), this lifestyle boutique remains the first port of call for Porto's style-conscious gents. The concept was born out of a collaboration between João Pedro Vasconcelos, CEO of Wrong Design, fashion director Miguel Flor and Lisbon architect Nuno Paiva, and Wrong Weather is an all-encompassing retail experience. Here, international brands and the in-house label are on sale alongside music, books and bikes, and there's a mezzanine art gallery exhibiting photography, painting and more. Nearby, Mercado 48 (T 22 323 9326) has a good range of eclectic locally made items, like glassware recycled from discarded bottles. *Avenida da Boavista 754, T 22 605 3929, www.wrongweather.net*

Livraria Lello

Frequently cited as one of the world's best bookshops, Lello is worth visiting simply for its extraordinary interior – a fusion of neo-gothic and neo-baroque. The store was designed by the engineer Xavier Esteves in 1906 to celebrate Porto's intellectual scene and showcase Lello, which at the time was one of the country's most distinguished publishing houses. The central feature is an organic, twisting, blood-red staircase, which wraps itself in a knot as it ascends. In the ceiling, supported by fan vaulting, is a magnificent stained-glass skylight that bears the company logo. A series of relief carvings depicting 19th- and 20th-century Portuguese literary heavyweights, such as Camilo Castelo Branco and Tomás Ribeiro, adorn the wooden panelling throughout.
Rua das Carmelitas 144, T 22 200 2037, www.livrarialello.pt

ESCAPES
WHERE TO GO IF YOU WANT TO LEAVE TOWN

Porto sits at the mouth of the Douro Valley, and the region has long offered top-quality viniculture tourism from working wineries such as Quinta do Vallado (Peso da Régua, T 25 431 8081), designed by Guedes + DeCampos. There is also a clutch of restaurants to rival anything in town, including culinary star Rui Paula's DOC (Estrada Nacional 222, Folgosa, T 25 485 8123), which is located in an elegant structure balanced on stilts in the river, by architects Miguel Saraiva. The valley gets more rugged as it nears Spain, and not far from the border is Camilo Rebelo and Tiago Pimentel's 2009 Museu de Arte e Arqueologia do Vale Côa (Vila Nova de Foz Côa, T 27 976 8260), which protects the area's Palaeolithic rock carvings within a brutal, but beautifully detailed, cantilevered building sliced into a hill.

A high-speed rail connection provides an easy link to Lisbon, but if you truly want to escape, it's a delightful journey through varied landscapes to Alentejo (opposite). Guimarães, the original capital of Portugal, is closer (around 55km), and its exquisitely preserved medieval core is a UNESCO World Heritage site. At the northern limits of Porto's metro, Vila do Conde boasts a 16th-century town centre and aqueduct, and is dominated by the fortress-like Santa Clara convent, although locals flock here for the great beaches and kicking nightlife. To the south, Espinho, laid out on a grid plan, is another seaside getaway with some fine art deco architecture.
For full addresses, see Resources.

São Lourenço do Barrocal, Alentejo
Amid olive groves and vineyards, the São Lourenço do Barrocal estate – owned by the same family for eight generations – is situated close to the Spanish border in the foothills of the Monsaraz, and is a village unto itself. Eduardo Souto de Moura has converted its whitewashed stone buildings into rooms and cottages, and carved out a bar/restaurant (above), all with stylishly low-key interiors by AnahoryAlmeida. The spa (overleaf) uses plant-based Susanne Kaufmann products, and has a cedarwood tub. There's also a seasonal outdoor pool, a winery – with tastings – orange grove and working stables. It's a four-hour drive from Porto; stop for lunch at the Gonçalo Byrne-designed Loggia (T 23 985 3076) in the historic riverside town of Coimbra.
Monsaraz, T 26 624 7140,
www.barrocal.pt

Spa, São Lourenço do Barrocal

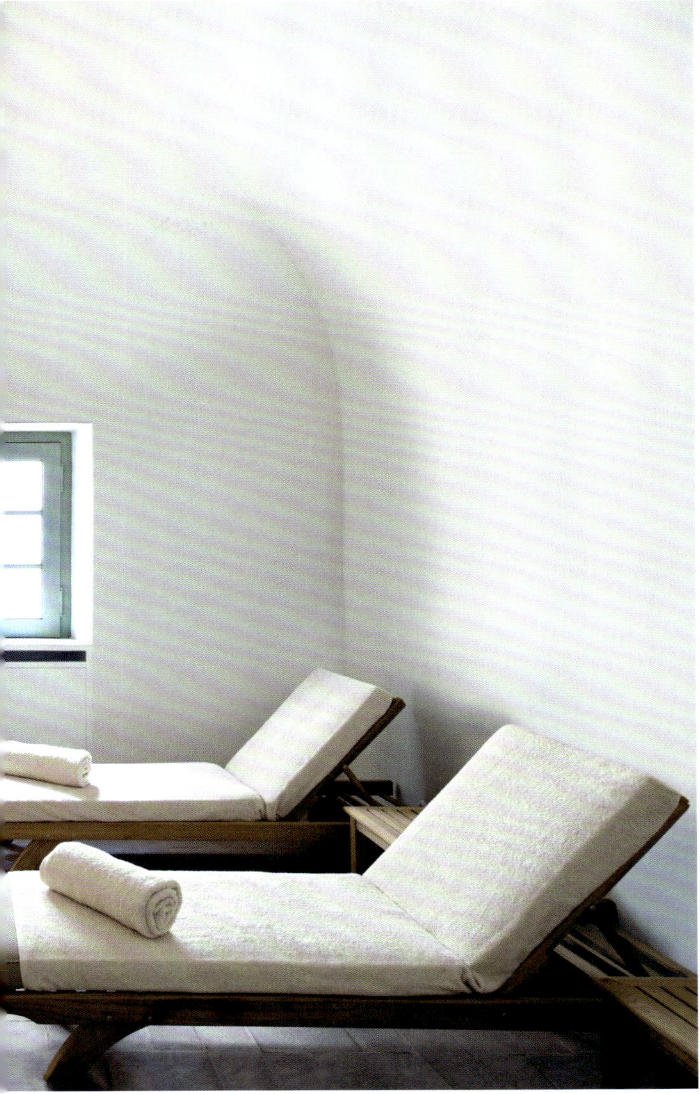

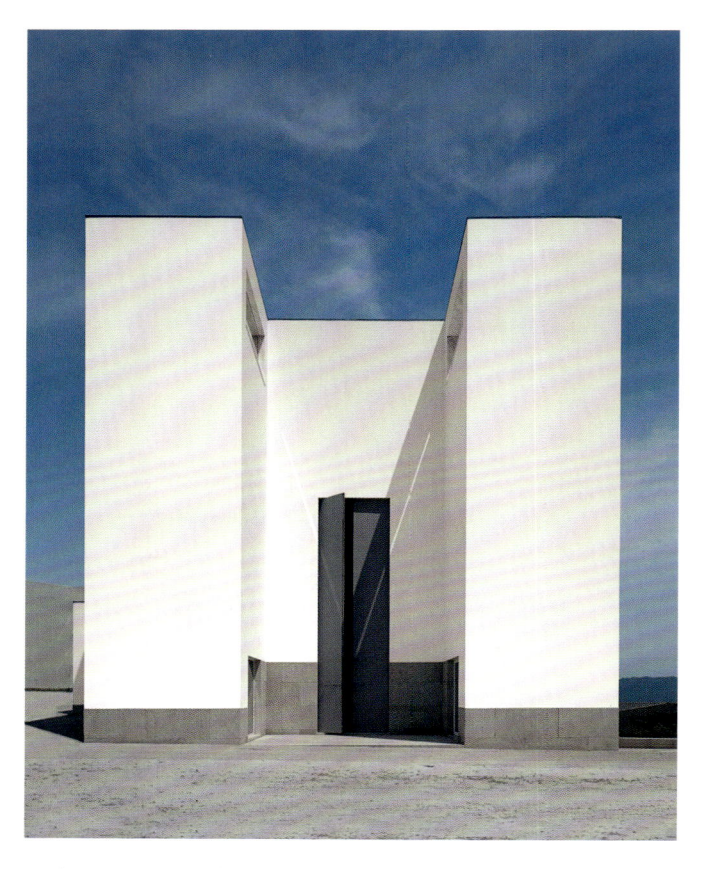

Igreja de Santa Maria, Tâmega
Sixty kilometres west of Porto, situated on the fringes of Marco de Canaveses, this 1997 church is among Siza Vieira's later works, which are characterised by white marble and render surfaces that decant natural light at varying times of the day, and impeccable levels of craftsmanship. Overlooked by suburban development, Santa Maria's environment is decidedly unpicturesque and the rather grandiose building is not Vieira's most sensitive, but it does command its context. The soaring interior is a sculptural space with a simple off-centre cross; exaggeratedly tall steel doors recall the boldness of Jørn Utzon; and there is a top-lit, tiled baptism area. A congregation of 400 can be seated on wooden chairs designed by Vieira himself.
Barrio dos Murteirados,
Marco de Canaveses

Pousada Mosteiro de Amares, Braga
Braga, 50km north of Porto, was once a stop-off point for pilgrims making their way to Santiago de Compostela in Spain. Legacies of this period are the Bom Jesus church, reached via a spectacular baroque staircase, and Santa Maria do Bouro, a 12th-century Cistercian monastery located just north of the city. Souto de Moura's superb 1997 overhaul is a lesson in how to convert historic structures for new uses (in this instance, the Pousada Mosteiro de Amares, an excellent 32-room hotel) and it's now a place of pilgrimage for architects and tourists. We never managed to prise ourselves away from the luxurious, stone-walled environs, which include a lovely pool and a cloistered bar, but the sporty may consider it a base for exploring the mountains of Peneda-Gerês national park.
Amares, T 25 337 1970, www.pousadas.pt

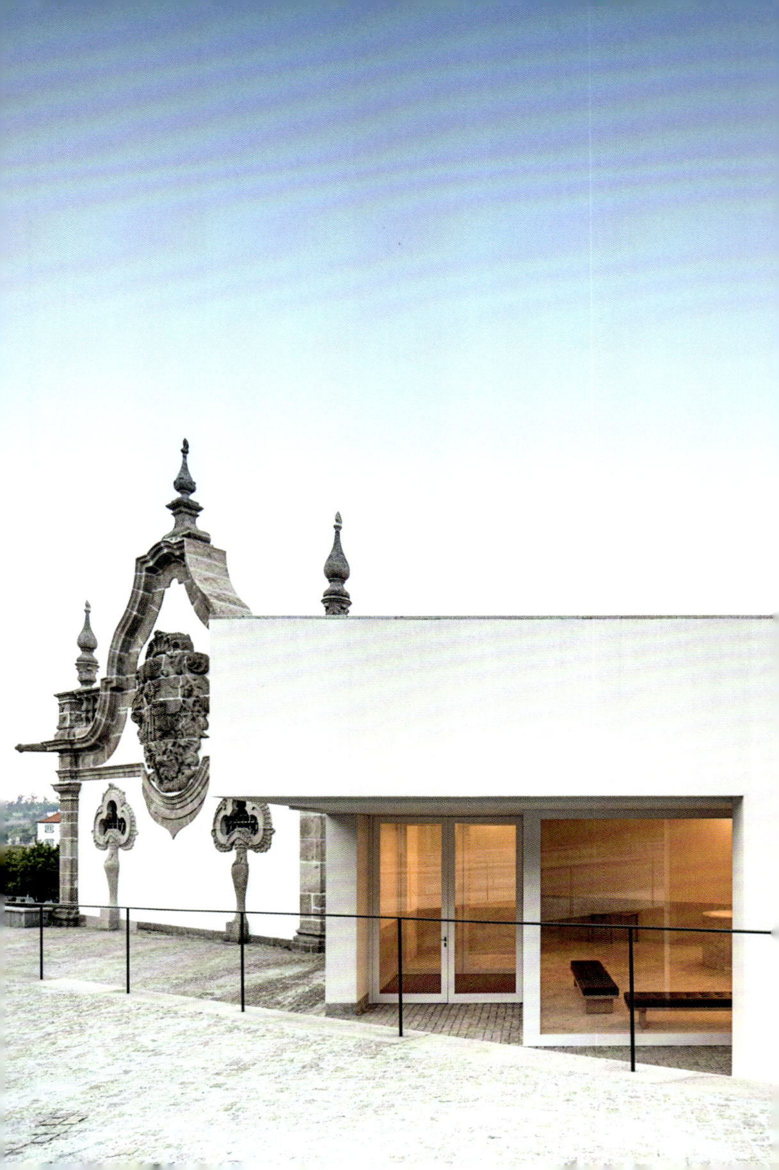

MIEC and MMAP, Santo Tirso
A 30-minute drive from Porto, the sleepy town of Santo Tirso is home to 54 large-scale sculptures that punctuate its public gardens. The artworks – including pieces by Ângelo de Sousa, Carlos Cruz-Diez and Mauro Staccioli – are part of the Museu Internacional Escultura Contemporânea (MIEC), which received a new HQ (opposite, right) in 2016, designed by the dream team of Souto de Moura and Siza Vieira. Beside the meticulously restored 18th-century monastery of São Bento, it is a sublimely minimal, low-slung wing that sits easily within its historic context. Consisting of a café as well as exhibition space, it shares an entrance with the Municipal Museum Abade Pedrosa (MMAP), which displays regional artefacts across seven rooms of the complex's former guesthouse (above).
Avenida Unisco Godiniz 100

NOTES
SKETCHES AND MEMOS

RESOURCES
CITY GUIDE DIRECTORY

A

Antiqvvm 088
 Rua de Entre Quintas 220
 T 22 600 0445
 www.antiqvvm.pt
Avenida 830 034
 Avenida da Boavista 830
 T 962 374 478
 www.avenida830.pt
A Vida Portuguesa 026
 Rua Galeria de Paris 20
 T 22 202 2105
 www.avidaportuguesa.com

B

Bairro da Bouça 074
 Rua da Boavista/Rua das Águas Férreas
La Bohème Entre Amis 051
 Rua Galeria de Paris 40
 T 22 201 5154
 www.laboheme.com.pt
Bop Café 050
 Rua da Firmeza 575
 T 22 200 1732
 www.bop.pt
Brasão Cervejaria 036
 Rua Ramalho Ortigão 28
 T 934 158 672
 www.brasao.pt
Breyner85 056
 Rua do Breiner 85
 T 22 201 3172
 www.breyner85.com

C

Café Candelabro 053
 Rua da Conceição 3
 www.cafecandelabro.com

Café Ceuta 052
 Rua de Ceuta 20
 T 22 200 9376
Café au Lait 032
 Rua Galeria de Paris 46
 www.cafeaulait-porto.blogspot.com
Café Vitória 042
 Rua José Falçao 156
 T 22 013 5538
 www.cafevitoria.com
Cafeína 039
 Rua do Padrão 100
 T 22 610 8059
 www.cafeina.pt
Cantinho do Avillez 041
 Rua Mouzinho da Silveira 166
 T 22 322 7879
 www.cantinhodoavillez.pt
Casa Almada 064
 Rua do Almada 544
 T 919 893 040
 www.casaalmada.com
Casa da Arquitectura 072
 Rua Roberto Ivens 582
 T 22 240 4663
 www.casadaarquitectura.pt
Casa da Música 010
 Avenida da Boavista
 T 22 012 0200
 www.casadamusica.com
Casa das Artes 028
 Rua Ruben Andresen 210
 T 22 011 6350
 www.casadasartes.pt

Casa de Chá da Boa Nova 027
Avenida da Liberdade
T 22 995 1785
Casa do Cinema Manoel de Oliveira 082
Rua Bartolomeu Velho
Casa d'Oro 046
Rua do Ouro 797
T 22 610 6012
www.restaurantecasanostra.com
Centro Comercial Bombarda 024
Rua Miguel Bombarda 285
T 934 337 703
www.ccbombarda.blogspot.com
A Certain Lack of Coherence 058
Rua dos Caldeireiros 77
T 919 272 115
www.acertainlackofcoherence.blogspot.com
Cinema Batalha 072
Praça da Batalha 47
T 22 201 1913
www.cinemabatalha.com
City Hall 009
Praça General Humberto Delgado
T 22 209 7135
Clérigos 009
Rua de São Filipe Nery
T 22 014 5489
www.torredosclerigos.pt
Cleriporto 088
Rua da Assunção 38
T 22 203 8027

Coliseu 076
Rua de Passos Manuel 137
T 22 339 4940
www.coliseu.pt
Cometa 054
Rua de Tomás Gonzaga 87
T 916 582 608
Confeitaria do Bolhão 025
Rua Formosa 339
T 22 339 5220
www.confeitariadobolhao.com
Confeitaria Império II 024
Rua de Fernandes Tomás 775
T 22 340 6187
Coração Alecrim 065
Travessa de Cedofeita 28
T 938 111 152
www.coracaoalecrim.com

D

Daily Day 090
Praça General Humberto Delgado 263
T 22 319 4583
www.daily-day.com
Dama Aflita 020
Rua de Picaria 84
www.damaaflita.com
DOC 096
Estrada Nacional 222
Folgosa
T 25 485 8123
www.ruipaula.com
D'Oliva al Forno 032
Rua Brito e Cunha 354
T 22 935 1005

E
Edifício Soares & Irmão 086
 Rua de Ceuta 16
Era Uma Vez no Porto 048
 Rua das Carmelitas 162
 T 22 202 2240
Espaço Mira 054
 Rua de Miraflor 159
 T 929 145 191

F
Faculdade de Arquitectura 084
 Via Panorâmica
 T 22 605 7100
 www.fa.up.pt
Fundação de Serralves 068
 Rua de Dom João de Castro 210
 T 22 615 6500
 www.serralves.pt

G
Galeria de Paris 024
 Rua Galeria de Paris 56
 T 22 201 6218
Galeria Fernando Santos 062
 Rua Miguel Bombarda 526
 T 22 606 1090
 www.galeriafernandosantos.com
Galeria Quadrado Azul 066
 Rua Miguel Bombarda 553
 T 22 609 7313
 www.quadradoazul.pt
Gare 054
 Rua da Madeira 182
 T 914 604 377
 www.gareporto.com
Góshò 016
 Porto Palácio
 Avenida da Boavista 1277
 T 22 608 6708
 www.gosho.pt

Gur 065
 T 912 307 453
 www.rugbygur.com

I
Igreja de Nossa Senhora da Boavista 077
 Rua Azevedo Coutinho 103
 T 22 600 2691
 www.paroquia-boavista.org
Igreja de Santa Maria 100
 Barrio dos Murteirados
 Marco de Canaveses
 Tâmega

K
Kubik Gallery 070
 Rua da Restauração 6
 T 22 600 4927
 www.kubikgallery.com

L
La Paz 092
 Rua da Reboleira 23
 T 22 202 5037
 www.lapaz.pt
Livraria Lello 095
 Rua das Carmelitas 144
 T 22 200 2037
 www.livrarialello.pt
Loggia 097
 Largo Doutor José Rodrigues
 Coimbra
 T 23 985 3076
 www.loggia.pt

M

Made In* 064
 Rua do Almada 331
 T 919 893 040
 www.casaalmada.com

Majestic 032
 Rua de Santa Catarina 112
 T 22 200 3887
 www.cafemajestic.com

Maus Hábitos 047
 Rua de Passos Manuel 178
 T 22 208 7268
 www.maushabitos.com

Mengos 024
 Rua de Santa Catarina 161
 T 22 200 3194

Mercado do Bolhão 088
 Rua Formosa

Mercado 48 094
 Rua da Conceição 48
 T 22 323 9326
 www.mercado48.pt

Mercearia do Miguel 035
 Rua do Passeio Alegre 130
 T 22 011 6889
 www.merceariadomiguel.com

Mercearia do Rosário 020
 Rua do Rosário 44
 T 22 201 0504

MIEC and MMAP 102
 Avenida Unisco Giniz 100
 Santo Tirso
 www.cm-stirso.pt

Miss'Opo 030
 Rua dos Caldeireiros 100
 T 22 208 2179
 www.missopo.com

Mondo Deli 033
 Rua do Almada 501
 T 22 203 3084
 www.mondo-deli.com

Mosteiro Serra do Pilar 009
 Vila Nova de Gaia
 Largo de Avis-Santa Marinha

Mundano Objectos 061
 Rua de Santos Pousada 668
 T 916 352 335
 www.mundano.pt

Múrias Centeno 058
 Rua Miguel Bombarda 531
 T 936 866 492
 www.muriascenteno.com

Museu de Arte e Arqueologia do Vale Côa 096
 Rua do Museo
 Vila Nova de Foz Côa
 T 27 976 8260
 www.arte-coa.pt

N

Nova Sintra Park 054
 Rua de Barão da Nova Sintra

O

Ó! Galeria 060
 Rua Miguel Bombarda 61
 T 930 558 047
 www.ogaleria.com

P

Passos Manuel 047
 Rua de Passos Manuel 137
 T 22 203 4121
 www.passosmanuel.net

Pavilhão Rosa Mota 085
Rua Dom Manuel II
T 22 543 0360
Pedras & Pêssegos 064
Rua do Almada 558
T 915 907 723
www.pedrasepessegos.com
Pedro Lemos 032
Rua do Padre Luís Cabral 974
T 22 011 5986
www.pedrolemos.net
Piscina das Marés 080
Leça da Palmeira
Avenida da Liberdade
T 22 995 2610
Piurra 056
Rua do Rosário 147
T 913 468 263
www.piurra.com
Plano B 054
Rua de Cândido dos Reis 30
www.planobporto.com
Ponte Luís I 013
Cais da Ribeira
Ponte Maria Pia 013
Avenida de Gustavo Eiffel
Portucale 044
Rua da Alegria 598
T 22 537 0717
www.miradouro-portucale.com

Q
Quem es, Porto? 057
Rua da Madeira
Quinta da Conceição 072
Avenida Doutor Antunes Guimarães
Quinta do Vallado 096
Peso da Régua
T 25 431 8081
www.quintadovallado.com

R
Rádio 036
Praça Dona Filipa de Lencastre 178
T 936 320 033

S
São Bento 072
Praça de Almeida Garrett
T 22 200 2722
Say My Name 089
Loja 7
Galerias Lumière
Rua José Falcão 157
T 932 479 184
www.saymyname.pt
Scar-ID 088
Rua do Rosário 253
T 22 203 3087
www.scar-id.com
Sé do Porto 009
Terreiro da Sé
T 22 205 9028
Silo-Auto 014
Rua de Guedes Azevedo 148-180

T
Taberna dos Mercadores 040
 Rua dos Mercadores 36-38
 T 22 201 0510
Terminal de Cruzeiros 073
 Avenida Comércio de Leixões
 T 22 999 0700
 www.apdl.pt
Torre Burgo 012
 Avenida da Boavista 1773
Traça 045
 Largo de São Domingos 88
 T 22 208 1065
 www.restaurantetraca.com

V
Vincci bar 038
 Alameda Basílio Teles 29
 T 22 043 9620
 www.vincciporto.com
Vodafone HQ 072
 Avenida da Boavista 2949

W
Wrong Weather 094
 Avenida da Boavista 754
 T 22 605 3929
 www.wrongweather.net

HOTELS
ADDRESSES AND ROOM RATES

Casa 1015 022
House:
Two people, from €115;
Four people, from €165;
Six people, from €225
Rua Padre Luís Cabral 1015
T 932 650 172
www.casa1015.pt

Infante Sagres 016
Room rates:
double, from €180
Praça Dona Filipa de Lencastre 62
T 22 339 8500
www.hotelinfantesagres.pt

Malmerendas 017
Room rates:
double, from €85;
Superior King Suite, €120
Rua Doutor Alves da Veiga
T 925 617 444
www.malmerendas.com

Miss'Opo Guesthouse 030
Room rates:
double, from €75
Rua de Trás 49
T 932 925 500
www.missopo.com

Palácio do Freixo 023
Room rates:
double, from €350;
Room 420, from €455
Estrada Nacional 108
T 22 531 1000
www.pestana.com

Pensão Favorita 020
Room rates:
double, from €90;
Room 5, from €90;
Room 6, from €95
Rua Miguel Bombarda 267
T 22 013 4157
www.pensaofavorita.pt

Pestana Vintage 016
Room rates:
double, from €160
Praça da Ribeira 1
T 22 340 2300
www.pestana.com

Porto Palácio 016
Room rates:
double, from €280
Avenida da Boavista 1269
T 22 608 6600
www.hotelportopalacio.com

Pousada Mosteiro de Amares 101
Room rates:
double, from €120
Largo do Terreiro
Santa Maria do Bouro
Amares
Braga
T 25 337 1970
www.pousadas.pt

Rosa et Al 018
Room rates:
double, from €190;
Queen Deluxe City Heritage Suite, €200;
Garden Pavilion, from €290
Rua do Rosário 233
T 916 000 081
www.rosaetal.pt

São Lourenço do Barrocal 097
Room rates:
double, from €155;
Two-person cottage, from €240
Monsaraz
Alentejo
T 26 624 7140
www.barrocal.pt

Sheraton 016
Room rates:
double, from €280
Rua Tenente Valadim 146
T 22 040 4000
www.sheratonporto.com

Vincci 036
Room rates:
double, from €125
Alameda Basílio Teles 29
T 22 043 9620
www.vincciporto.com

The Yeatman 016
Room rates:
double, from €185
Rua do Choupelo
T 22 013 3100
www.the-yeatman-hotel.com

WALLPAPER* CITY GUIDES

Executive Editor
Jeremy Case

Author
Syma Tariq

City Editor
Belle Place

Photography Editor
Rebecca Moldenhauer

Junior Art Editor
Jade R Arroyo

Editorial Assistant
Catalina L Imizcoz

Contributors
David Knight
Francesca Savoldi

Interns
Josie Finlay
Eleanor Hall
Emily Paul

Production Controller
Nick Seston

Marketing & Bespoke Projects Manager
Nabil Butt

Wallpaper*® is a registered trademark of Time Inc (UK)

First published 2011
Revised and updated
Second edition 2016

© Phaidon Press Limited

All prices and venue information are correct at time of going to press, but are subject to change.

Original Design
Loran Stosskopf
Map Illustrator
Russell Bell

Contacts
wcg@phaidon.com
@wallpaperguides

More City Guides
www.phaidon.com/travel

PHAIDON

Phaidon Press Limited
Regent's Wharf
All Saints Street
London N1 9PA

Phaidon Press Inc
65 Bleecker Street
New York, NY 10012

Phaidon® is a registered trademark of Phaidon Press Limited

www.phaidon.com

A CIP Catalogue record for this book is available from the British Library.

All rights reserved. No part of this publication may be reproduced, stored in a retrieval system or transmitted, in any form or by any means, electronic, mechanical, photocopying, recording or otherwise, without the prior permission of Phaidon Press.

Printed in China

ISBN 978 0 7148 7329 9

PHOTOGRAPHERS

João Morgado
Malmerendas, p017
Rosa et Al, p018, p019
Casa 1015, p022
Casa das Artes, p028, p029
Miss'Opo, pp030-031
Mondo Deli, p033
Avenida 830, p034
Mercearia do Miguel, p035
Rádio, pp036-037
Vincci bar, p038
Cafeína, p039
Taberna dos Mercadores, p040
Cantinho do Avillez, p041
Café Vitória, p042, p043
Traça, p045
Bop Café, p050
La Bohème Entre Amis, p051
Estelita Mendonça, p055
Quem es, Porto?, p057
Ó! Galeria, p060
Mundano Objectos, p061
Galeria Fernando Santos, pp062-063
Galeria Quadrado Azul, pp066-067
Kubik Gallery, pp070-071
Piscina das Marés, p080, p081
Say My Name, p089
Daily Day, pp090-091
La Paz, p092
MIEC and MMAP, p102, p103

Roger Casas
Porto city view, inside front cover
Casa da Música, pp010-011
Torre Burgo, p012
Ponte Maria Pia, p013
Silo-Auto, pp014-015
Palácio do Freixo, p023
Confeitaria do Bolhão, p025
A Vida Portuguesa, p026
Casa de Chá da Boa Nova, p027
Portucale, p044
Casa d'Oro, p046
Passos Manuel, p047
Era Uma Vez no Porto, pp048-049
Café Ceuta, p052
Café Candelabro, p053
Fundação de Serralves, p069
Bairro da Bouça, pp074-075
Coliseu, p076
Igreja de Nossa Senhora da Boavista, p077, pp078-079
Casa do Cinema Manoel de Oliveira, pp082-083
Faculdade de Arquitectura, p084
Pavilhão Rosa Mota, p085
Edifício Soares & Irmão, p086, p087
Wrong Weather, p094
Livraria Lello, p095

Jade R Arroyo
La Paz shirt, p093

Duccio Malagamba
Igreja de Santa Maria, p100

PORTO
A COLOUR-CODED GUIDE TO THE HOT 'HOODS

MATOSINHOS
The main harbour was moved to this beautifully rugged stretch of coast in the 1970s

FOZ DO DOURO
Wealthy Portuenses have always made their homes where the Douro meets the Atlantic

BOAVISTA/CEDOFEITA
The Casa da Música concert hall is a must-see and the nearby boutiques are top-notch too

SANTO ILDEFONSO
This delightful residential district comes as a surprise so close to the bustling Downtown

LORDELO DO OURO/SERRALVES
One of the top contemporary art collections in the country draws the crowds to Serralves

CLÉRIGOS/DOWNTOWN
The old town is a joy to explore and its steep lanes are home to hip bars and restaurants

MASSARELOS
Architectural gems here include Pavilhão Rosa Mota and Siza Vieira's university buildings

GAIA
Cross one of Porto's many bridges for spectacular city views and its legendary wine caves

For a full description of each neighbourhood, see the Introduction.
Featured venues are colour-coded, according to the district in which they are located.